THE ADDISON–WESLEY NETWORKING BASICS SERIES

EIG

The Addison-Wesley Networking Basics Series

The Addison-Wesley Networking Basics Series is a set of concise, hands-on guides to today's key technologies and protocols in computer networking. Each book in the series covers a focused topic and explains the steps required to implement and work with specific technologies and tools in network programming, administration, and security. Providing practical, problem-solving information, these books are written by practicing professionals who have mastered complex network challenges.

Tom Clark, *Designing Storage Area Networks: A Practical Reference for Implementing Fibre Channel SANs*, 0-201-61584-3

Gary Scott Malkin, *RIP: An Intra-Domain Routing Protocol*, 0-201-43320-6

Geoff Mulligan, *Removing the Spam: Email Processing and Filtering*, 0-201-37957-0

Alvaro Retana, Russ White, and Don Slice, *EIGRP for IP: Basic Operation and Configuration*, 0-201-65773-2

Richard Shea, *L2TP: Implementation and Operation*, 0-201-60448-5

John W. Stewart III, *BGP4: Inter-Domain Routing in the Internet*, 0-201-37951-1

Brian Tung, *Kerberos: A Network Authentication System*, 0-201-37924-4

Andrew F. Ward, *Connecting to the Internet: A Practical Guide about LAN-Internet Connectivity*, 0-201-37956-2

Visit the Series Web site for new title information:
http://www.awl.com/cseng/networkingbasics/

THE ADDISON–WESLEY NETWORKING BASICS SERIES

EIGRP for IP

Basic Operation and Configuration

Alvaro Retana
Russ White
Don Slice

Addison–Wesley

Boston • San Francisco • New York • Toronto • Montreal
London • Munich • Paris • Madrid
Capetown • Sydney • Tokyo • Singapore • Mexico City

Many of the designations used by manufacturers and sellers to distinguish their products are claimed as trademarks. Where those designations appear in this book, and we were aware of a trademark claim, the designations have been printed in initial capital letters or all capital letters.

The authors and publisher have taken care in the preparation of this book, but make no expressed or implied warranty of any kind and assume no responsibility for errors or omissions. No liability is assumed for incidental or consequential damages in connection with or arising out of the use of the information or programs contained herein.

The publisher offers discounts on this book when ordered in quantity for special sales. For more information, please contact:

Pearson Education Corporate Sales Division
One Lake Street
Upper Saddle River, NJ 07458
(800) 382-3419
corpsales@pearsontechgroup.com

Visit AW on the Web: www.awl.com/cseng/

Library of Congress Cataloging-in-Publication Data

Retana, Alvaro.
    EIGRP for IP : basic operation and configuration / Alvaro Retana, Russ White, Don Slice.
        p. cm. —(Addison-Wesley networking basics series)
    Includes bibliographical references and index.
    ISBN 0-201-65773-2
     1. Routers (Computer networks) 2. Computer network protocols.
I. White, Russ. II. Slice, Don. III. Title. IV. Series.
   TK5105.543. R48 2000
   004.6′2—dc21   00–027094

Copyright © 2000 by Addison-Wesley

All rights reserved. No part of this publication may be reproduced, stored in a retrieval system, or transmitted, in any form or by any means, electronic, mechanical, photocopying, recording, or otherwise, without the prior written permission of the publisher. Printed in the United States of America. Published simultaneously in Canada.

ISBN 0-201-65773-2
Text printed on recycled paper.
1 2 3 4 5 6 7 8 9—MA—0403020100
First printing, May 2000

Contents

Preface	ix
Chapter 1: EIGRP Fundamentals	**1**
Distance Vector and Link State Protocols	1
Distance Vector Protocols	1
Link State Protocols	5
EIGRP Compared to Other Protocols	6
EIGRP: The Basics	8
Neighbor Relationships	8
Reliable Multicast	9
Limiting Bandwidth Consumption	12
EIGRP's Foundation: DUAL	13
The Metric	15
A More Practical Example	16
Split Horizon and Queries	17
Queries with No Feasible Successor	20
Where Does the Query End?	21
Deciding Where to Use EIGRP	22
Chapter 2: EIGRP Configuration	**23**
Starting and Running EIGRP	23
The `network` Command	23
The Autonomous System (AS) Number	25
Redistribution	25
Externals and Internals	26
Caveats	27
Configuring Summarization	28
Autosummarization	28
Manual Summarization	29
Distribution Lists	31
Standard Access Lists as Distribution Lists	31
Extended Access Lists as Distribution Lists	32
Hello and Hold Timers	33

Logging Neighbor Status	34
Passive Interface	34
Stub Neighbors	35

Chapter 3: EIGRP Network Design — 37

Network Topology	37
Hierarchy	38
Redundancy	39
Minimizing Query Range	41
Summarization	42
Route Filtering	45
Stub Routers	47
Multiple Autonomous Systems	48
Multiple Routing Protocols	49
Path Selection Issues	50
Changing the Metric Components on an Interface	50
Offset Lists	52
Changing K Values	53
Variance	55
Asymmetric Routing	57
Default Routing Strategy	58
WAN and Dial Issues	62
Frame Relay and Bandwidth Statements	62
Point-to-Point Subinterfaces	64
Multipoint Interfaces and Subinterfaces	64
Dual-Homed Remotes	67
Low-Speed NBMA Links and SIAs	69
NBMA and Split Horizon	72
Frame-Relay Broadcast Queue	72
Dial Backup Strategies	74
Redistribution Issues	76
General Issues	77
Forms of Redistribution	80
Administrative Distance	82
Source of Redistributed Routes	84
Other Design Considerations	91

Chapter 4: EIGRP Troubleshooting   95

Problems with Neighbor Relationships   95
    One-Way Communication between Two Routers   96
    Unicast-Only between Two Routers   97
    Multicast-Only between Two Routers   99
    Overburdened or Dirty Link   100
Stuck in Active Routes   101
    Why Did the Route Go Active?   101
    Why Did the Route Stay Active So Long?   102
Duplicate Router IDs   104
Failure to Converge   107
    Simplifying the Network   107
    Isolate Misbehaving Routers   107
    Diagnose the Event   108

Glossary   109
Recommended Reading   117
Index   119

Preface

Cisco Systems designed EIGRP (Enhanced Interior Gateway Routing Protocol) to support the Internet Protocol (IP), Novell's IPX, and Apple's AppleTalk protocols. EIGRP is used in networks of all sizes, including many large corporate networks, across the world. Routers direct traffic—user data in the form of packets—through the network toward its destination. Routing protocols provide the road signs for the routers to use to decide where to forward the traffic to next on the path to the destination.

EIGRP is designed to provide routing knowledge within a single domain—or between routers controlled and maintained by the same group of people. A domain is usually understood as containing all the routers owned and operated by a single administration, such as a company or a department.

Although EIGRP can provide routing information for various protocols, we have limited the scope of this book to just IP. The primary reason for this decision is to maintain focus and clarity. Most of the theory and the design principles you learn here can be applied to networks using EIGRP to route protocols other than IP.

This book has been designed to provide a quick but complete description of EIGRP and its use. Throughout our experience, working firsthand on the design and troubleshooting of EIGRP networks, we have found that the protocol is typically not well understood or documented. Although EIGRP is very easy to configure, the lack of educational resources explaining how EIGRP functions has led to nonoptimized networks and has caused issues to chronically pop up in many of them. Our intent is to partially fill the documentation gap with this guide while also providing design and troubleshooting guidelines to the most common scenarios and problems. The intended audience includes people with some networking experience and at least a basic understanding of routing protocols.

Chapter 1 begins with EIGRP theory, explaining the basic concepts, terminology, and mechanisms EIGRP uses to provide routing information. Chapter 2 takes a brief look at the most important configuration options with EIGRP. Chapter 3 considers network design principles within the framework of EIGRP's capabilities and includes tips on basic network architecture and specific studies on situations you may find in an EIGRP network. Finally, Chapter 4 provides information on troubleshooting various conditions you may find within a network running EIGRP. Problems ranging from errors building neighbor relationships to troubleshooting Stuck in Active (SIA) routes are covered in this chapter.

In this book, key terms appear in **boldface** type the first time they are used. These terms are defined in the glossary at the end of the book, following Chapter 4.

Acknowledgments

We would like to thank the people at Addison-Wesley, especially Mary Hart, for their patience while pushing this project along through the long effort involved in writing a book. We would also like to thank our colleagues at Cisco and our reviewers, without whom this project would not have been possible. Their comments and corrections helped us improve the content of this book. Many thanks to all our reviewers: Louis Breit, Rick Burts, Eric Herrin, Glen Herrmannsfeldt, Craig Partridge, John Stewart, and Jessica Yu.

Alvaro Retana: I want to thank my parents for giving me an education and teaching me the meaning of hard work and responsibility. This is for my wife, Dora, who has always supported and encouraged me.

Russ White: I'd like to thank my wife, Lori, who puts up with me through the turmoil of writing books, and my daughter, Rebekah, who plays by herself when I'm busy writing (not too often or long, of course). I'd like to thank my stepfather, Harvey Russ, for pushing me into computers in the first place. (Thanks for the XT.) Finally, and most important, I would like to thank God for giving me the talent, opportunities, and faith to do things like this.

Don Slice: I would like to give special thanks to my wife, Pam, for her understanding and love, even when I'm stressed with deadlines and overwork. She keeps everything together while I'm busy running in circles. I'd also like to thank my daughters, Jessica, Amy, and Heather, for being patient and for loving me even when I'm too busy trying to get things done to give them the attention they deserve. And most of all, I'd like to thank God for His love and strength.

1

EIGRP Fundamentals

Cisco's EIGRP (Enhanced Interior Gateway Routing Protocol) is an advanced **distance vector protocol** based on **DUAL (Diffusing Update Algorithm)**. In this book, we will explain EIGRP's operation, explore network design, and cover troubleshooting for common problems.

Just in the first paragraph, we've introduced concepts that need clarification; we've said EIGRP is *enhanced* and *advanced*. In this first chapter, we'll try to clarify these concepts by covering the fundamental workings of EIGRP, keeping in mind that this book has been designed to provide quick answers to common configurations and problems rather than an in-depth study of the protocol. To put EIGRP in perspective, we will first briefly discuss the operation of two prevalent types of routing protocols.

Distance Vector and Link State Protocols

Routing protocols can generally be classified as either *distance vector* or *link state;* several well-known implementations of these two types of protocols are common in most networks. In this section, we'll discuss the basic characteristics of both and present some of EIGRP's unique traits. A more detailed discussion of EIGRP is presented later in this chapter.

Distance Vector Protocols

The most common distance vector protocol is **RIP (Routing Information Protocol)**. When someone says a protocol is a distance vector protocol, most people think "periodic updates and slow convergence." Although some distance vector protocols, such as RIP and Cisco's **IGRP**

(**Interior Gateway Routing Protocol**), do converge slowly and use periodic updates, these aren't the defining attributes of a distance vector protocol.

The main characteristic of a distance vector protocol—and what distinguishes it from a **link state protocol**—is that each node in the network advertises all the destinations it knows about to its directly attached neighbors. This reachability information is announced in the form of a *distance*—the cost of reaching a particular destination—and a *vector*—the direction packets should take to reach the destination. In other words, like a sign in the highway, the advertisement indicates the destination, the distance, or cost, to get there, and the direction to take. As with the highway sign, no information is given about the topology of the network, although some clues can be inferred from the number of hops, or the cost. We'll use Figure 1.1 and walk through how some of this process works.

Updates: If the routers in this network are running a distance vector protocol, they will advertise the information they know to *all* their directly attached neighbors. Obviously, C would initially be the only router that knows how to reach 10.1.1.0/24. C will advertise this information to B and D, which in turn will advertise it to A—and back to C. When it receives an advertisement, or **update,** a router increments the **metric** to reflect the cost of traversing the link between itself and its neighbor. *Any paths other than the best path are discarded*. Although C receives an update from both B and D that contains a route to 10.1.1.0/24, C discards them because they have a higher metric than the route to the directly connected interface the destination is attached to.

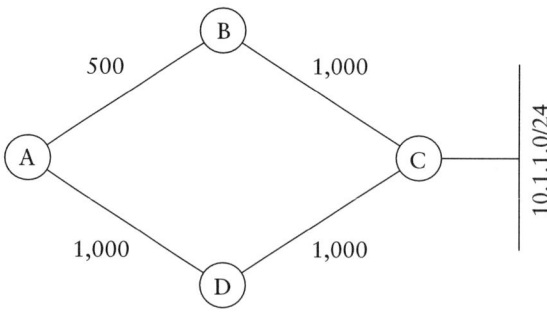

Figure 1.1 A simple network

In RIP and IGRP, the advertisements are periodic, so it will take a multiple of the advertisement interval—90 seconds in IGRP's case—for information to be propagated across the network. This sounds pretty slow to us! Each router learns the direction toward the destination from the advertising neighbor: Router A can reach 10.1.1.0/24 through either B or D. This algorithm—advertise everything known to all directly connected neighbors and choose the path with the best metric—is known as the Bellman-Ford algorithm.

Periodic updates affect not only the initial information transmission but also the propagation of changes. In some distance vector implementations, after a change is detected, the protocol must wait until the periodic timer expires to advertise the new information.

Furthermore, the network may fall into a *count-to-infinity* problem in which two or more nodes enter in a routing information loop until the cost reaches the maximum value. In RIP, *infinity* is reached when a hop count of 16 is arrived at; protocols with a composite metric, such as IGRP and EIGRP, have a much higher concept of *infinity*. Bear in mind updates are sent—after incrementing the metric—to *all* the neighboring nodes. As an example, assuming that the cost on all the interfaces is 1, C would advertise the route to 10.1.1.0/24 with a metric of 1, and nodes B and D would advertise the route with a metric of 2.

Consider a failure scenario in which C loses its interface to 10.1.1.0/24; C will still receive updates from B and D with a metric of 2—and in this case, 2 is the best metric! B and D, having lost their best route, will now prefer the metric of 3, advertised by both A and C, and will advertise a metric of 4. Both A and C will now use the route with a metric of 4 as their preferred path and will advertise a metric of 5. This process will repeat itself until *infinity* is reached. Because the advertisements may be periodic, *counting to infinity* may take quite a long time. Common techniques aimed at preventing count-to-infinity routing loops are **holddown, split horizon,** and **poison reverse**. Later in this book, we will cover specifics on how they affect EIGRP's operation.

Unlike some implementations of RIP and IGRP, EIGRP doesn't use periodic updates. Instead, EIGRP uses **incremental updates,** which means that changes are propagated immediately. The use of incremental updates speeds the initial information transfer and decreases the time for change data to reach the whole network.

EIGRP also doesn't discard unused path information but instead keeps it in a **topology database**. DUAL, which is used in EIGRP, uses the information in the topology database to find alternative loop-free paths that will be used in case the main path is no longer present. DUAL and the protocol's behavior when changes occur are described later.

Metrics: Throughout this book, the terms *cost, distance,* and *metric* are used to indicate the same thing. RIP uses hops as its metric; each node in the network represents 1 hop. The maximum number of hops is 16, thereby limiting the size of the network. In Figure 1.1, for example, the distance to 10.1.1.0/24 from A would be 2 hops: through either B or D.

IGRP and EIGRP may use up to four different parameters to calculate the cost: **bandwidth, delay, load,** and **reliability**. The following formula calculates the metric in IGRP:

$$metric = \left\langle \left[(K_1 * bandwidth) * \frac{(K_2 * bandwidth)}{256 - load} \right] + (K_3 * delay) \right\rangle * \left(\frac{K_5}{reliability + K_4} \right)$$

By default, the value for the constants is $K_1 = K_3 = 1$, and $K_2 = K_4 = K_5 = 0$. Furthermore, the *bandwidth* is the normalized value (with respect to 10^7) of the minimum bandwidth (in kilobits per second) in the path to the destination. The *delay* is the sum of the delays (in microseconds) in the path. Substituting these values into the formula and reducing it results in

$$\left(\left(\frac{10^7}{min(bandwidth)} \right) + \sum delays \right)$$

If you followed along and did the algebra, you've noticed that with $K_5 = 0$, reducing this formula always results in 0. EIGRP bends the rules of algebra a bit and ignores the entire last term if $K_5 = 0$.

The use of a composite metric—one made up of more than one variable—allows for having a better criterion for selecting the best path. A higher cost can be assigned to slower paths.

Link State Protocols

Link state protocols have been considered an improvement to solve some of the problems encountered with distance vector protocols: slow convergence, count to infinity, and so on. **OSPF (Open Shortest Path First)** and **IS-IS (Intermediate System to Intermediate System)** are examples of widely deployed link state protocols.

Routers running a link state protocol advertise only their local information but do so to *all* the other routers in the network. Each router is responsible for announcing information about the state of the links—attached subnets and neighbors—it is directly connected to. The updates are incremental, with a periodic refresh, and are flooded throughout the network by sending them to a **multicast** address. Each node makes a local copy of the link state packet and forwards it.

A network implementing a link state protocol can be thought of as a jigsaw puzzle, as shown in Figure 1.2. The link state information that each node originates represents a piece of the puzzle. Once any node has all the pieces, it may calculate the shortest path, or lowest cost, to any given destination.

The flooding mechanism distributes the information, guaranteeing that all nodes receive it. The Dijkstra algorithm is used to calculate a tree—with the local node as the root—from this information and finds a loop-free path to every destination. As you can imagine, this method of finding the shortest path can be very CPU intensive, especially as the

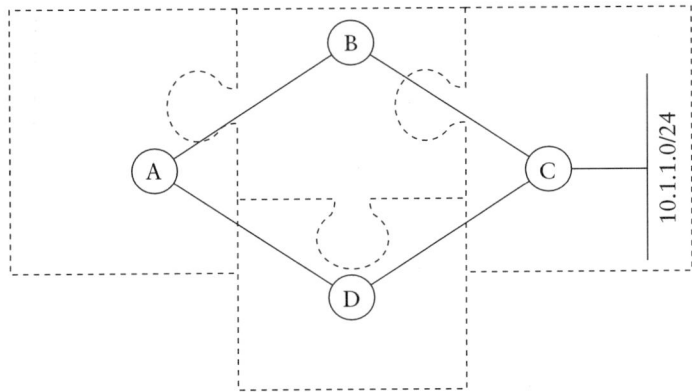

Figure 1.2 A simple network: jigsaw puzzle

size of the tree increases. Link state protocols introduce the concept of *areas* to reduce the sizes of the trees; areas are network regions that must have the same topology database. Areas represent logical boundaries for the flooding of link state information.

Areas also complicate and limit link state protocols. In general, areas must be built in a hierarchy, and filtering and **summarization** can be done only at area boundaries or at the node where the information originated. Distance vector protocols—and EIGRP specifically—provide more flexibility by allowing filtering and summarization at any point in the network.

As far as metrics is concerned, OSPF uses the link bandwidth to calculate the cost. IS-IS uses an arbitrary cost.

EIGRP Compared to Other Protocols

We've covered quite a bit of ground so far. Here's a short comparison of EIGRP with other protocols on various dimensions.

Algorithm:

- RIP/RIPv2: Bellman-Ford distance vector
- IGRP: Bellman-Ford distance vector
- OSPF: Dijkstra link state
- IS-IS: Dijkstra link state
- EIGRP: DUAL distance vector

Metric:

- RIP/RIPv2: hop count
- IGRP: based on bandwidth and delay
- OSPF: based on bandwidth
- IS-IS: arbitrary cost
- EIGRP: based on bandwidth and delay

Chapter 1: EIGRP Fundamentals

Updates:

- RIP: periodic full updates to a **broadcast** address
- RIPv2: periodic full updates to a multicast or broadcast address
- IGRP: periodic full updates to a broadcast address
- OSPF: flooding as needed and periodically to a multicast address
- IS-IS: flooding as needed and periodically to a multicast address
- EIGRP: updates and queries as needed to a multicast address

Loop prevention:

- RIP/RIPv2: split horizon and holddown timers
- IGRP: split horizon and holddown timers
- OSPF: full knowledge of **topology**
- IS-IS: full knowledge of topology
- EIGRP: split horizon and DUAL

Convergence:

- RIP/RIPv2: holddown and wait for alternative paths to be advertised
- IGRP: holddown and wait for alternative paths to be advertised
- OSPF: rerun Dijkstra with modified database
- IS-IS: rerun Dijkstra with modified database
- EIGRP: DUAL, possible use of alternative known loop-free routes or queries to neighbors for alternative-path information

Other features:

- RIP: **classful;** filtering possible on any router; no summarization within a major network
- RIPv2: **classless;** and otherwise similar to RIP
- IGRP: classful; filtering possible on any router; no summarization within a major network

- OSPF: classless; filtering and summarization possible on Autonomous System Border Routers (ASBRs) or Area Border Routers (ABRs)

- IS-IS: classless; filtering and summarization possible when a route is injected into the network or at a level boundary

- EIGRP: classless; filtering and summarization possible anywhere in the network

EIGRP: The Basics

Although the mathematical basis for EIGRP is complex, the protocol is easy to configure and to run in small and large networks. In this section, we walk through neighbor relationships, reliable multicast, and limiting bandwidth consumption. We'll then look at how DUAL works, the metrics, and, finally, the query process.

Neighbor Relationships

EIGRP relies on **neighbor** relationships to provide reachability information. Having learned information from a neighbor, a router assumes that the information is valid as long as the neighbor relationship stays intact. If the information does change, the advertising neighbor is required to transmit a **query,** an update, or another indication of the change. In other words, EIGRP has no periodic routing updates.

These neighbor relationships are formed and maintained through *hello* packets. Each router periodically transmits hello packets to a multicast address on each attached link. Any other router that receives these hello packets will note a new neighbor and will begin the process of advertising routes to it. The first update packet the router sends to this new neighbor will have an initialization bit set, letting the new neighbor know that it needs to start sending back any routing information it has.

If it doesn't hear a hello from a neighbor within the **hold time,** a router will assume that the neighbor is no longer there and will remove any topology information received from that neighbor. It is important

Chapter 1: EIGRP Fundamentals   **9**

to mention that the *hold* timer is reset when any packet—not just a *hello* packet—from a neighbor is received.

How often are hello packets sent, and how long is the hold time? The answers depend on the link type speed.

- For all **point-to-point link** types, including **HDLC (high-level data link control)** serial links, **frame relay point-to-point subinterfaces,** and others, the hello timer is 5 seconds, and the hold timer is 15 seconds.

- For all links with a bandwidth over 1,000,000 (approximately T1 speed), the hello timer is 5 seconds, and the hold timer is 15 seconds; this category includes all **LAN (local area network)** media.

- For all **multipoint** links with a bandwidth less than 1,000,000 (approximately T1 speed), the hello timer is 60 seconds, and the hold timer is 180 seconds.

The hello and hold timers on either end of a link don't need to match for a neighbor relationship to be built, because the hold time is included in the hello packet itself. A router will use the hold time advertised by its neighbor to determine how long it should wait without hearing any hello packets before declaring the neighbor down.

Reliable Multicast

A routing protocol can send updates and other information between routers in three ways:

- **Unicast,** which is how **BGP (Border Gateway Protocol)** works, as well as EIGRP and OSPF in some situations

- Broadcast, which is the way the RIPv1 works

- Multicast, which is the way EIGRP, IS-IS, and OSPF work

Multicast is more efficient than broadcast because the packets can be filtered by most network interface chips rather than being passed up to the IP layer to be sorted. EIGRP uses the multicast address 224.0.0.10, which translates to the **MAC (media access control) address** 01-00-5E-00-00-0A.

In order to ensure that routing updates and queries are not lost, we need a way to make certain other routers have received these multicast packets intact and to recover from errors if they haven't. For these reasons, updates and queries are handled by the **reliable multicast** transport in EIGRP.

Let's use Figure 1.3 to discuss how the process works. We'll go through a very simple case, and then we'll work through a failure scenario.

- A sends out some information that both B and C need to receive. A sends this information to the EIGRP multicast address.

- B receives the information and sends a unicast **acknowledgment** back to A.

- C receives the information and sends a unicast acknowledgment back to A.

Simple, right? Updates and queries are sent as multicast packets, and the receiving router always acknowledges their receipt, using a unicast packet. What if A sends out a packet, B replies, but C never does? How long would A wait before doing something to recover, and what would A do?

How long will a router wait before starting the recovery mechanism? Each time it sends out a multicast packet that must be reliably delivered, an EIGRP process will wait until the **RTO (retransmission timeout)** period has passed before beginning a recovery action. This period is calculated from the **SRTT (smooth round-trip time)**, which is

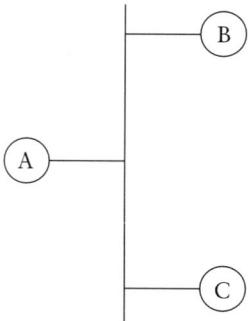

Figure 1.3 Reliable multicast in EIGRP

Chapter 1: EIGRP Fundamentals

calculated as the amount of time taken in the past for each peer on an interface to respond.

The values of the SRTT and the RTO depend on quite a few parameters, including the number of neighbors on the interface, the number of retransmissions attempted, and the bandwidth configured on the interface. As these parameters vary dynamically, so does the formula to calculate the SRTT and the RTO. In the simple case of two neighbors on a point-to-point interface, the RTO is typically six times the SRTT; the value may vary from a minimum of 200 microseconds (ms) to a maximum of 5 seconds (s). These timers are shown in the output of the `show ip eigrp neighbor` command.

```
router#show ip eigrp neighbor
IP-EIGRP neighbors for process 100
  H  Address          Interface    Hold Uptime   SRTT  RTO   Q   Seq
                                   (sec)  (ms)               Cnt Num
  0  16.1.1.3         Se0            13  00:00:25  100  4500  0   1
```

How does the router recover from a failed multicast? If a router sends out a multicast packet and never receives an acknowledgment, what action does the router take? First, the router makes a list of all the neighbors from which it did not receive an acknowledgment. Second, the router sends out a packet telling those neighbor routers that didn't respond not to listen to multicast until they've been notified that it's safe again: that recovery is complete. Third, the router will begin sending unicast packets with the information to the routers that didn't answer, continuing until they've caught up.

Let's work through a more practical example, using the network depicted in Figure 1.3 as an example.

1. A sends out an update or a query, a type of multicast packet that must be delivered reliably.
2. B responds with an acknowledgment, but C doesn't respond.
3. A waits for the neighbor for the period of time specified in the RTO.
4. Once this time period has passed, A sends out an unreliable-multicast packet, called a *sequence TLV* (type-length-value) packet, which tells C not to listen to multicast packets any longer.

5. A then continues sending any other multicast traffic it has and delivering all traffic, using unicast packets to C, until it acknowledges all the outstanding packets.
6. Once C has "caught up," A will send another sequence TLV, telling C to begin listening to multicast again.

Steps 4 and 5 are repeated until node C has received all the outstanding information. The sequence TLV packet contains a list of the nodes that should not listen to multicast packets while the recovery takes place. The packet sent in step 6 does not contain any nodes in the list.

While recovering, each reliable multicast packet transmitted has the CR (conditional receive) bit set to indicate that it should be processed only if the receiving node's address was not present in the preceding sequence TLV packet. The CR bit is also useful if node C can receive multicast packets only intermittently; the CR bit guarantees that the node will not process the reliable-multicast packet if the sequence TLV packet was not received.

How long will the router continue attempting to recover from a failed reliable multicast? Once a router drops back into unicast transmissions, it won't keep trying forever to get the information transmitted. A router will either (1) attempt to retransmit the unicast 16 times, waiting longer to try again each time it retransmits or (2) continue to retransmit until the hold timer for the neighbor in question expires. Once it has been sending retransmissions for the longer of these two periods of time—16 retries or the hold time for the neighbor—a router will declare a *retransmission limit exceeded* error and will reset the neighbor.

What is transmitted using reliable multicast? The types of packets that warrant the attention the reliable-multicast system provides are updates and queries. Hellos, acknowledgments, and sequence TLVs are sent unreliably; that is, they don't require acknowledgments.

Limiting Bandwidth Consumption

One of the problems facing protocols that send routing information only on demand is that they can consume all the bandwidth available exchanging routing information while trying to converge. EIGRP resolves the problem of bandwidth starvation by consuming only up to 50 percent—the default value—of the bandwidth available on a link. (The amount of bandwidth that EIGRP is allowed to consume is configurable.)

EIGRP accomplishes this by pacing its packets. Essentially, the process is:

- Calculate how long it takes to send a single bit on the link.
- Multiply that number by the size of the packet ready to be sent.
- Wait this amount of time—or a portion/multiple of this time, depending on the configuration—before sending the packet.

What bandwidth is used for the calculation of this pacing interval? Again, it is the bandwidth that is configured on the interface. Refer to Table 3.1 for a list of the default bandwidths for some common interfaces on Cisco routers.

It's always best to manually configure the bandwidth for what the line rate really is—or the committed information rate for links that have a clock rate different from the signal rate—rather than just use the default. This is particularly true for serial links, which almost always default to 1.544 and almost always have a lower real bandwidth. On multipoint (not broadcast) interfaces, the bandwidth available is divided by the number of neighbors reachable through the interface, to compensate for the lower link speeds that are likely at the remote ends of the links.

EIGRP's Foundation: DUAL

The foundation of EIGRP is the Diffusing Update Algorithm, or DUAL, a method of finding loop-free paths through a network, proposed by J. J. Garcia-Luna. We will discuss the theory behind DUAL before diving into how EIGRP has implemented it.

The fundamental concept behind DUAL is as follows: *It is mathematically possible to determine whether any route is loop free, based on the information provided in standard distance vector routing.* In other words, DUAL can determine which path to a destination is loop free, in a way that is independent of choosing which path to use. Let's go into a practical example, based on Figure 1.4.

Assume that A is trying to find the best path, or lowest cost, to 10.1.1.0/24. A traditional distance vector protocol, such as RIP or

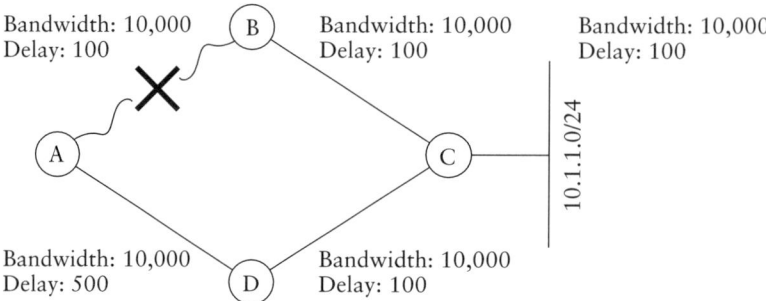

Figure 1.4 A simple DUAL example

IGRP, would simply add the cost of each link and choose the best path. The remaining paths would be discarded because the protocol assumes that worse paths are possible loops and should be avoided. It's clear from Figure 1.4 that A has two loop-free paths available: one through B and the other one through D.

Using the following process, DUAL will quickly determine that these two paths are both valid:

- Compare the cost of the two paths and select the lowest; this cost is called the **feasible distance (FD)**. The neighbor advertising this path to the destination becomes the **successor**. The total cost of the path is obtained by adding the cost to reach the neighbor—1,000 to reach node D from node A, for example—to the metric advertised by that neighbor.

- The metric advertised by the *successor* is called the **reported distance (RD),** or the distance the neighbor is reporting to the router performing DUAL. In this case, the *reported distances* through B and D are both 1,000.

- In any case, where the *reported distance (RD)* is less than the *feasible distance (FD)*, the path is considered loop free. Any neighbor that meets this criterion becomes a **feasible successor (FS)**.

It is mathematically provable that any path with an RD that is less than the FD will be loop free, but we'll leave that as an exercise for the reader.

The Metric

With these basics in hand, we can begin to look at how EIGRP implements DUAL. The metrics are integral to the remainder of the discussion, so let's approach them first.

As discussed earlier, EIGRP builds on the metrics used in IGRP. The basic information used to build the EIGRP metric is provided by the bandwidth and the delay, and the formula used to compute the metric is

$$\left(\left(\frac{10^7}{\min(bandwidth)}\right) + \sum delays\right) * 256$$

One question that often arises when people see the formula is: Why multiply by 256? Wouldn't it be simpler just to compute things as they are? Well, yes. But remember that EIGRP uses the IGRP metric as its reference point and that IGRP uses a 24-bit number—2^{24} is its maximum metric—to represent the distance to a destination. EIGRP's designers wanted to use 32 bits to add granularity to the metric. The simplest way to use the 32 bits was to shift the existing IGRP metric left by 8 bits, which is equivalent to multiplying it by 256.

> One thing that can be confusing when you are dealing with EIGRP metrics is that the metric calculated by the router will often not be the metric you would find if you did the calculations by hand. The reason for this apparent mistake is that Cisco routers do not perform floating-point operations but instead round down when calculating the total EIGRP metric at various points in the formula.

Although EIGRP also keeps the path **MTU (maximum transmission unit)**, link **reliability,** and link load in the topology table and can be configured to use this information when calculating the best path, none of these other metrics can trigger an update, so they aren't very useful. In other words, EIGRP will not recalculate the best path based on the load of the links in the path alone: Something else must change to prompt EIGRP to recalculate the path metric before it will notice that the load on the path has changed. We would recommend, therefore, that the other metrics shouldn't ever be used, and we won't discuss how to use them.

When advertising a destination, EIGRP uses bandwidth and delay as they are configured on the router's interface. In other words, the delay is not measured in real time or anything like that. The value assigned to the delay depends on the default bandwidth on the interface (see Table 3.1 for some sample values). The delay can also be configured independently of the bandwidth, using the interface-level `delay` command.

A More Practical Example

Figure 1.5 shows the same network as in Figure 1.4 but this time with a little more realistic metrics assigned to the links. Let's use this network to determine what router A would have in its topology table and what happens when one of the two paths to the network attached to router C fails.

The first thing to do when figuring out which path A will choose is to see what metric A will calculate for each path.

- The path through B will be $((10^7 / 10{,}000) + 100 + 100 + 100)256$, which is 332,800.

- The path through D will be $((10^7 / 10{,}000) + 200 + 100 + 100)256$, which is 358,400.

So A will choose the path through B as the best path and will route traffic in that direction. Now, will A believe that the path through D is loop free? Let's calculate the RDs to see.

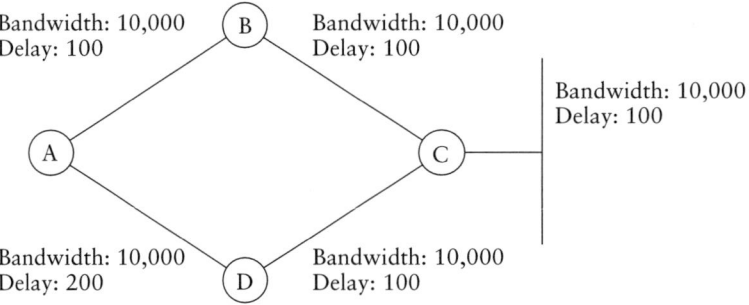

Figure 1.5 A simple network, using real metrics

- The RD from B will be $((10^7 / 10{,}000) + 100 + 100)256$, which is 307,200.

- The RD from D will be $((10^7 / 10{,}000) + 100 + 100)256$, which is 307,200.

Is the RD through D less than the FD (the metric through the best path)? Yes, 307,200 is less than 332,800. So A will believe that the path through D is loop free and will mark it as a feasible successor (FS) in its topology table.

Let's take a look at what A will do if the path through B fails (Figure 1.6). When the link fails between A and B, router A will immediately recognize that its best path to the network attached to C is no longer valid and will search its topology table for another loop-free path to this destination. Because A has another loop-free path, the path through D, A will begin using this path.

Split Horizon and Queries

So far, we've dealt with a very simple case: two paths, one of which is an FS of the other. In reality, few cases are this simple, and we have to contend with *split horizon*.

Split horizon is the rule that *a router should not advertise a path to a destination through the interface it is using to reach that destination.* (Let's call this interface the upstream interface.) Split horizon is used in all

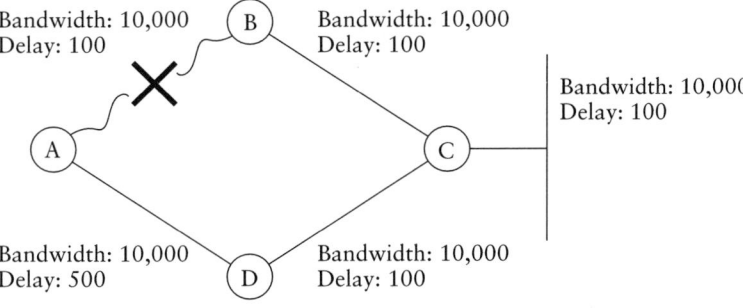

Figure 1.6 Losing the best path in the simple network

distance vector protocols to speed convergence. The theory behind split horizon is as follows: There's no need to advertise the cost to the destination in the upstream direction, because the cost should be higher. In other words, the upstream routers should already have a lower-cost path available. In many cases, the use of split horizon in distance vector protocols reduces the **convergence time** by avoiding the *count-to-infinity* problem.

EIGRP also uses split horizon. In some cases, it may contribute to DUAL's not finding an alternative loop-free path, even if one exists. Let's modify our simple network slightly to provide an example in which split horizon has an influence on DUAL (Figure 1.7).

Let's begin with D rather than A, as that's where the action is this time. D will compute

- The path through A as $((10^7 / 10{,}000) + 100 + 100 + 100)256$, which is 332,800
- The path through C as $((10^7 / 1{,}000) + 5{,}000 + 100)256$, which is 3,865,600

So D will choose the path through A as its successor. Computing the RDs, we find that

- The RD from A is $((10^7 / 10{,}000) + 100 + 100)256$, which is 307,200.
- The RD from C is $((10^7 / 10{,}000) + 100)256$, which is 281,600.

Because 281,600, the RD through C, is less than 332,800, the FD, or the best path, the path through C will be marked as an FS in D's topology

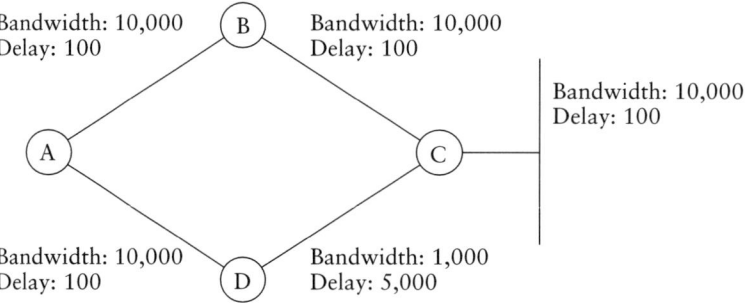

Figure 1.7 A simple network with split-horizoned routes

table. Because D is using the path through A, D will not advertise that it can reach the network attached to C toward A; it will apply split horizon to it. A will have only one path to the network attached to C: through B.

Let's look at what happens if the path between A and B fails now (Figure 1.8). When the link between A and B fails, A finds that it has no other path to the destination network. In other words, node A does not have a feasible successor in its topology table. How does A find the valid alternative path? When a topology change occurs, EIGRP actively searches for an alternative path to any destinations impacted by the change. EIGRP searches for alternative paths by sending query packets to all its neighbors, asking them whether they know of a different path to the destination. The query process allows EIGRP to converge quickly in many circumstances, but it can also create significant activity if a serious trauma occurs. (More details on how to avoid or minimize problems are presented later in the book.) In steady state, all entries in the topology table are marked as **passive;** during the query process, affected routes are marked as **active**. Queries are sent to all the neighbors except the ones that advertised the active route.

A will send a query to D, which will examine its topology table and discover that although it has now also lost its best path, it does have another loop-free path, an FS, through C for this destination. D will reply with this information, and the network will converge with the path through D as the only path. It is important to mention that if node D didn't have a feasible successor, it would also send a query to all its neighbors (except A, in this example).

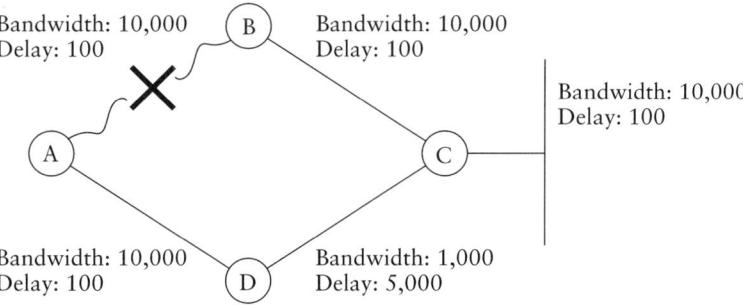

Figure 1.8 Convergence in a network with split-horizoned paths

Queries with No Feasible Successor

Although we've presented a simple case in which queries come into play, there are other cases. Changing the metrics in the sample network, we could make it so that A uses B as its primary path, D uses C as its primary path, but the path through D doesn't appear to be loop free from A's perspective (Figure 1.9).

Let's calculate the metrics and RDs as A sees them.

- The path through B has a metric of 332,800 and an RD of 307,200.
- The path through D has a metric of 409,600 and an RD of 358,400.

Because the RD through D is higher than the best path, the FD, the path through D is not considered loop free and is therefore not marked as an FS in A's topology table. From D's perspective,

- The path through A has a metric of 384,000 and an RD of 332,800.
- The path through C has a metric of 358,400 and an RD of 281,600.

So the path through A is a feasible successor, with the best path being through C. Note that D is not using the path through A, so it will not split horizon; it will advertise the destination network to A.

In this situation, if the link between A and B fails, A will examine its topology table and find that it knows another path. A suspects that the alternative path contains a loop, so it will mark the route active and will query its neighbors for other paths to the destination.

Because D is using the path through C as its best path (successor), it will reply to A with the metric for the path through C. Once A has

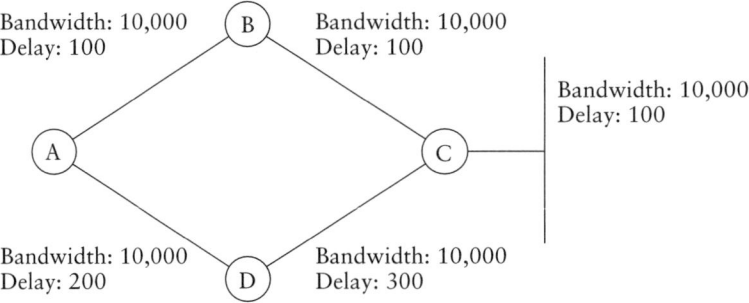

Figure 1.9 Queries with no feasible successor

received replies for all its queries, it will see that C has replied with a valid alternative path and will begin using it. In Chapters 3 and 4, we present an in-depth analysis of issues that have to be taken into account for the successful completion of the query process.

Where Does the Query End?

Queries may cascade throughout a network, stopping only when one of three conditions is met:

- An alternative path is found.
- The end of the network is reached.
- Information about the network that is the subject of the query is unknown.

When it receives a query, a router may give three answers.

- If it receives a query about a route and has an alternative path that doesn't go through the router asking the question (a feasible successor), a router will immediately answer with the metric it uses to reach the target. It doesn't need to send queries to anyone else, because it has no need to search for another path; it already has one.
- If a router receives a query and has no one else to ask, it immediately replies with an answer of infinity or unreachable, meaning the destination isn't reachable through this router.
- If a router receives a query about a route not contained in its topology table, it immediately answers with an infinity reply or unreachable.

The last property is extremely important to understand when designing an EIGRP network and is the subject of much of the discussion presented in Chapter 3.

When it sends a query to its neighbors, a router sets a timer for approximately 3 minutes (it could be as high as 3½ minutes) and must receive replies to all queries before the timer expires. If the timer expires, the route is considered **SIA (Stuck in Active)**, and the peering with the neighbor that didn't answer is reinitialized. However, reinitialization of the neighbor relationships is not something you want to happen regularly on your network. Occasional SIA routes will happen on most EIGRP networks of significant size and are not any reason to be alarmed. SIA routes are, however, an indication of problems on the network; if they happen too frequently, SIAs will greatly reduce a network's stability.

Deciding Where to Use EIGRP

Probably the most frequently asked question for not only EIGRP but also any protocol is: What protocol should I use in my network? What protocol is best? The answer to these and similar questions is very simple: It depends!

Some of EIGRP's main traits that should be considered when selecting a protocol for your network are

- Cisco-proprietary protocol
- Classless protocol
- Filtering and summarization possible at any point in the network
- Distance vector protocol
- Incremental updates
- Query process used to find alternative paths

This list is in no way an indication that if any or all of these characteristics can be accommodated, you should use EIGRP in your network; it's just a short summary of things to keep in mind when making your decision.

You will find that EIGRP has some strong points and some weak ones, as any protocol used for carrying routing information does. There is no "silver bullet" in the world of routing protocols, just good design coupled with choosing the right tool for the job. In many large networks, EIGRP performs quickly, puts minimal strain on the network, and allows a great deal of flexibility.

2

EIGRP Configuration

With the theory out of the way, we can move on to more practical matters, such as how to configure EIGRP. This chapter covers getting the protocol going, configuring summaries and summary methods, logging various state changes, and using other configuration options you might encounter. The commands and configurations discussed here are for Cisco routers (the only routers that support EIGRP). We'll hold off on design concepts and issues in relation to these configuration options until Chapter 3.

Starting and Running EIGRP

Starting EIGRP on a Cisco router is very simple; two commands will suffice. To start EIGRP running with an **AS** (**autonomous system**) number or process ID of 100 for the 10.0.0.0/8 network, we could type

```
router(config)#router eigrp 100
router(config-rtr)#network 10.0.0.0
```

The `network` Command

The `network` command, however, is a bit deceptive and needs some further explanation. Oblivious to the keyword used in the command itself—network—the `network` command doesn't determine what the router will advertise. Instead, the `network` command determines which interfaces EIGRP will run on. We won't build neighbor relationships or exchange routes over an interface with an IP address that isn't included in a `network` command.

How does the router determine what to advertise? The router collects the IP address and subnet masks of every interface that has an IP address included through a `network` command and builds a list of connected subnets that need to be advertised.

This may seem like a distinction without a difference, or just plain confusing, until you reach Cisco's IOS version 12.0(4)T, when EIGRP begins accepting wildcard bits rather than just major networks in the `network` command. With the wildcard bits, you can configure EIGRP to run on a single interface or all interfaces, without any regard to the major network the interfaces are in.

To make this a little more clear, let's use the following set of interfaces and their assigned IP addresses to work through a couple of examples:

- Ethernet 0 with an IP address of 10.1.1.1/25
- Ethernet 1 with an IP address of 10.1.1.129/25
- Ethernet 2 with an IP address of 10.2.8.65/26
- Serial 0 with an IP address of 172.16.1.1/24
- Serial 1 with an IP address of 172.16.2.1/24

Then, for each of the following configuration requirements, we could use the indicated configuration commands:

- Run EIGRP on all interfaces in the 10.0.0.0 network:

```
router eigrp 100
  network 10.0.0.0
```

- Run EIGRP only on interface Ethernet 0:

```
router eigrp 100
  network 10.1.1.1 0.0.0.0
```

- Run EIGRP on interfaces in the 10.1.1.0/24 range of addresses:

```
router eigrp 100
  network 10.1.1.0 0.0.0.255
```

- Run EIGRP on Ethernet 0 and serial 0 only:

```
router eigrp 100
  network 10.1.1.1 0.0.0.0
  network 172.16.1.1 0.0.0.0
```

- Run EIGRP on all the interfaces on the router:

```
router eigrp 100
  network 0.0.0.0 0.0.0.0
```

The wildcard bits don't act like a subnet mask at all. They don't need to be contiguous; nor do they indicate the subnet of any IP address anyplace on the router. They simply mark out a range of addresses to be included, similar to the wildcard bits used in building access lists on Cisco routers. The addition of wildcard bits in the `network` command provides a great deal more flexibility in configuring EIGRP, including the ability to support a supernetted IP address—a CIDR (classless interdomain routing) block on a single interface.

The Autonomous System (AS) Number

The number required after the `router EIGRP` command is the AS number and/or the *process ID*. EIGRP routers configured with different ASs will not form neighbor relationships or exchange routes. To exchange routes between routers in different ASs, you must redistribute between them. Although we will talk about the commands to perform redistribution between different ASs here, we wouldn't recommend that you design a network with multiple EIGRP ASs, for reasons we discuss in Chapter 3.

Redistribution

Redistribution into and out of EIGRP is also straightforward to configure. The redistribution must be configured, and then the EIGRP process has to be told what metric to use when advertising the routes it has learned from the external source. The redistributed metric can be configured in two ways: as part of the `redistribution` command itself or in a separate `default-metric` command.

For instance, suppose that we wanted to redistribute routes being learned from another routing protocol running on a router. Using RIP as an example, we could configure

```
router eigrp 100
        redistribute rip metric 10000 100 255 1 1500
```

The five number elements listed after the `metric` keyword are the bandwidth, delay, reliability, load, and maximum transmission unit (MTU). Even though only the bandwidth and the delay are used when calculating the metrics, all five are required for redistribution to work properly.

Another option is to enter the metric separately:

```
router eigrp 100
  redistribute rip
  default-metric 10000 100 255 1 1500
```

Here, the `default-metric` command is used to configure the metrics EIGRP should use for all routes redistributed into AS 100, regardless of their source.

Externals and Internals

Routes that have been redistributed into EIGRP are considered **external routes**. The **AD (administrative distance)** of these routes is different from that of internal EIGRP routes; internal EIGRP routes will always be preferred over external EIGRP routes. EIGRP externals carry a large amount of information in the route, such as the originating **router ID**, the originating protocol, the originating protocol's metric, and an administrative tag.

The administrative tag is set and checked, using route maps, while in the process of redistributing a route. For example, to set an administrative tag, you could use

```
route-map set-tag permit 10
  set tag 100
!
router eigrp 100
  redistribute rip route-map set-tag
```

Chapter 2: EIGRP Configuration

Then, to check for the existence of a given tag, you could use

```
route-map check-tag permit 10
  match tag 10
```

Administrative tags will prove useful in handling externals when we discuss redistribution design (Chapter 3).

Caveats

- *Redistribution on Cisco routers is always done from the routing table.* A route that isn't the routing table cannot be redistributed. This is important, because changing the administrative distance on EIGRP externals can have disasterous effects on redistribution by introducing routing loops into the network.

- *Metrics don't always need to be supplied when redistributing into EIGRP.* If the protocol that is being redistributed into EIGRP uses metrics that are comparable to EIGRP metrics, the metrics will be accepted from the other protocol. The only protocol that uses metrics comparable to EIGRP's metrics is IGRP. So, to shorten the rule, if you are redistributing from EIGRP into EIGRP or from IGRP into EIGRP, you don't need to configure redistribution metrics.

- *Any directly connected route will be advertised as an internal if there is a network statement that includes the route.* For example, consider the following configuration:

```
router eigrp 100
  network 10.1.1.0 0.0.0.255
!
ip route 10.1.1.0 255.255.255.0 ethernet0
```

The route 10.1.1.0/24 will be advertised as an internal EIGRP route as long as the Ethernet 0 interface is up. This may seem odd when you first look at it, but it's because the router places static routes to interfaces in the routing table as connected destinations.

Configuring Summarization

EIGRP has two types of summarization: manual and automatic. The two are configured in completely different ways.

Autosummarization

Autosummarization is an EIGRP feature that makes migration from fully classful protocols, such as RIP or IGRP, easier and that also provides a base level of summarization in your network. Autosummarization summarizes to classful boundaries each time a major network boundary is crossed, with one exception.

For example, in the network shown in Figure 2.1, autosummarization would take place at two points. Here, given that all these routes are internal:

- B will summarize the 10.1.1.0/24 and 10.1.2.0/24 networks to 10.0.0.0/8 toward C *and* the 192.168.1.0/25 network into 192.168.1.0/24 toward A.

- C will summarize the 172.16.1.0/24 network into 172.16.0.0/16 toward B.

In each of these cases, EIGRP will also create a summary route in its topology table, pointing to `NULL0`, and will install that route into the routing table with an administrative distance of 5. This effectively emulates classful routing behavior: Any packets destined to a subnet within a major network for which the router has no path will be dropped.

One important exception is that external routes are not autosummarized. Going back to the network in Figure 2.1, let's assume that C has a `redistribute connected` statement configured rather than a `network`

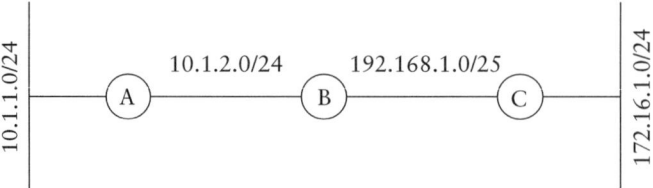

Figure 2.1 Autosummarization in EIGRP

Chapter 2: EIGRP Configuration

statement for the Ethernet interface on 172.16.1.0/24. Because it is redistributed into EIGRP, 172.16.1.0/24 will be an external, and externals are not autosummarized. C will not build a summary for the 172.16.0.0/16 major network; it will advertise the 172.16.1.0/24 external component instead.

To further confuse matters, if autosummarization is taking place for another internal component of a given network, externals within the same major network will be included within the summary. Let's look at Figure 2.2 for an example of this. Here, let's assume that C is redistributing 172.16.1.0/24 into EIGRP, whereas B has a `network` statement for its interface on the 172.16.2.0/24 network. C will not build a summary for the 172.16.0.0/16 network, but B will, and it will advertise that summary toward both A and C. To support discontiguous subnets, you will need to turn autosummarization off by configuring `no auto-summary` within the EIGRP routing process.

Manual Summarization

EIGRP also allows you to summarize at any point in the network to any prefix length, using the `ip summary-address` command on individual interfaces. This feature is extremely useful in truly hierarchical network designs with good addressing, because you can cut down on routing table sizes dramatically. Let's use the network in Figure 2.3 to see how EIGRP can be configured to summarize routes.

Let's assume that you would like to configure a summary so that the only route advertised from B toward C is 10.1.0.0/16. The configuration would look something like this:

```
interface Serial0
  ip summary-address eigrp 100 10.1.0.0 255.255.0.0
!
router eigrp 100
  network 10.0.0.0
```

This would cause B to create a route to 10.1.0.0/16 via `Null0`:

```
router#show ip route
. . . .
D       10.1.0.0/16 is a summary, 00:00:03, Null0
. . . .
```

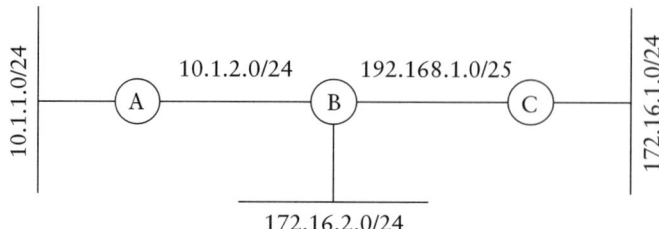

Figure 2.2 Autosummarization with mixed internals and externals

We could also see this by looking at the EIGRP topology table:

```
router#show ip eigrp topology 10.1.0.0 255.255.0.0
IP-EIGRP topology entry for 10.1.0.0/16
State is Passive, Query origin flag is 1, 1 Successor(s), FD
  is 128256
  Routing Descriptor Blocks:
  0.0.0.0 (Null0), from 0.0.0.0, Send flag is 0x0
  Composite metric is (128256/0), Route is Internal
    Vector metric:
      Minimum bandwidth is 10000000 Kbit
      Total delay is 5000 microseconds
      Reliability is 255/255
      Load is 1/255
      Minimum MTU is 1514
      Hop count is 0
```

The summary route created by EIGRP has, by default, an administrative distance of 5. If this route overlaps with another route you wanted to leave intact, you can set the administrative distance for the

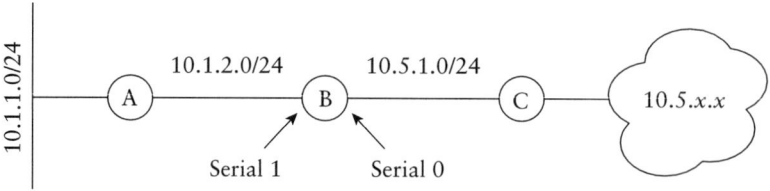

Figure 2.3 Manual summarization in EIGRP

Chapter 2: EIGRP Configuration

summary route using the administrative distance option at the end of the `ip summary-address` command.

For instance, if we wanted to advertise a default route from B toward A without overriding any default route that B may already be learning from elsewhere, we could configure

```
interface Serial1
   ip summary-address eigrp 100 0.0.0.0 0.0.0.0 200
```

Unlike autosummarization, manual summaries will summarize all internal and external destinations that fall into the range of addresses configured.

Distribution Lists

Another important capability in any routing protocol is the ability to block the distribution of routes beyond a certain point. EIGRP allows you to block routes by using distribution lists at any point in the network. Two forms of access lists can be used as distibution lists: standard IP access lists and extended IP access lists. Let's use Figure 2.4 to work through examples, using both of these types of access lists.

Standard Access Lists as Distribution Lists

In Figure 2.4, we want to prevent either B or C from learning about the 172.16.1.0/24 network. The configuration required is relatively easy:

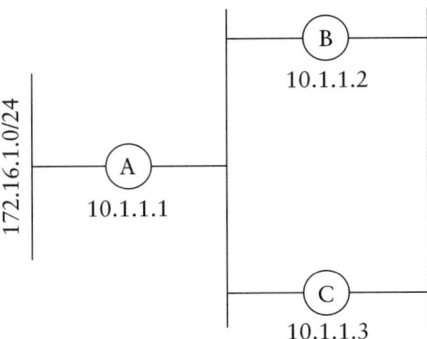

Figure 2.4 Distribution lists

```
hostname A
!
access-list 10 deny 172.16.0.0 0.0.255.255
access-list 10 permit any
!
router eigrp 100
  network 10.1.1.1 0.0.0.0
  network 172.16.1.0 0.0.0.255
  distribute-list 10 out
```

There is also an option to block the advertisement of the route out one interface only.

```
hostname A
!
access-list 10 deny 172.16.0.0 0.0.255.255
access-list 10 permit any
!
interface Ethernet0
  ip address 10.1.1.1 255.255.255.0
!
router eigrp 100
  network 10.1.1.1 0.0.0.0
  network 172.16.1.0 0.0.0.255
  distribute-list 10 out ethernet0
```

This configuration allows the 172.16.0.0/16 network to be advertised to every other interface except Ethernet 0.

Extended Access Lists as Distribution Lists

It's also possible to use extended access lists as distribution lists within EIGRP. It's a little puzzling when you first approach it, as an extended access list has two IP addresses and two wildcard masks: one that is normally used for the source and one that is normally used for the destination. The first network address and wildcard are used to specify the networks affected by the list. But what are the second IP address and wildcard mask used for? They are used to indicate the *source* of the advertisement.

Chapter 2: EIGRP Configuration

For example, if we wanted B to learn about the 172.16.0.0/16 network through A but didn't want C to learn about this network through A, we could configure

```
hostname C
!
access-list 150 deny ip 10.1.1.1 172.16.1.0 0.0.0.255 host
   10.1.1.1
access-list 150 permit ip any any
!
router eigrp 100
  network 10.1.1.0 0.0.0.255
  distribute-list 150 in
```

Now C would accept all advertisements for networks within the 172.16.0.0 range except those from A. (Note that it will learn of this network through B across their shared Ethernet, anyway.) This type of configuration would be useful, perhaps, in enforcing a policy that traffic to a certain destination shouldn't pass between two given routers or, perhaps, in some firewall situations.

Hello and Hold Timers

It's sometimes useful to be able to set the hello and hold timers on a given interface running EIGRP; in fact, there is one situation in which we would recommend that you set these timers to something other than the default values, which we will cover in Chapter 3. Configuring these timers is straightforward, with one small side note: Configuring one timer will not affect the other. Setting the hello timer to 10 seconds won't automatically set the hold timer to 30 seconds; nor will setting the hold timer have any effect on the hello timer. These two timers must be set independently to values that make sense for the network and the design requirements at hand.

To configure these timers, use the `ip hold-time` and `ip hello-time` configuration commands. For instance, to configure the hello timer to 10 seconds and the hold timer to 30 seconds, you could use

```
router(config)#interface serial 0
router(config-int)#ip hello-time eigrp 100 10
router(config-int)#ip hold-time eigrp 100 30
```

Logging Neighbor Status

By default, EIGRP gives you little to no information about changes in neighbor status. Because this status is so important to judging the health of a network running EIGRP and is crucial for troubleshooting a network failure after the dust has settled, we would highly recommend that all routers in your network be configured to log their neighbor changes to the console or other logging facility.

The configuration needed to log these status changes is very simple:

```
router eigrp 100
  eigrp log-neighbor-changes
```

Configure this on each and every router running EIGRP in your network!

Passive Interface

You may want to configure a network statement that includes a given interface but then not run EIGRP on that interface. This is true, for instance, when you want a given destination to be included as an internal route within the EIGRP routing domain but you don't want EIGRP to send hellos or other packets on the interface. For instance, looking back at Figure 2.4, if we wanted A to advertise the 172.16.1.0 network but not run EIGRP on that interface, we could configure

```
router eigrp 100
  network 172.16.1.0 0.0.0.255
  passive-interface ethernet0
```

It's also possible to mark all interfaces passive and then specify which interface to run EIGRP on. Again going back to Figure 2.4, we could configure all interfaces passive and then specifically instruct EIGRP to run on the serial interface:

```
router eigrp 100
  network 0.0.0.0 0.0.0.0
  passive-interface default
  no passive-interface serial0
```

Stub Neighbors

The ability to configure a neighbor as a **stub** has only recently been added to EIGRP. This feature is *very* useful when trying to reduce the query range in a network with a lot of dual-homed remotes (see Chapter 3 for more information). Configuring a stub router is simple; on the router you don't want to receive queries (the remote router), configure

```
router eigrp 100
  network 0.0.0.0 0.0.0.0
  neighbor x.x.x.x stub <connected|summary|external>
```

The options at the end of the command allow you to determine what types of routes this router will advertise to the neighbor specified.

- The `connected` option causes only routes derived from interfaces directly connected to this interface to be advertised.

- The `summary` option causes only summary routes created on this router to be advertised.

- The `external` option causes routes redistributed into EIGRP on this router to be advertised.

These options may be used in combination; the default is to specify `connected` and `summary`.

3

EIGRP Network Design

EIGRP has proved itself a flexible, reliable protocol if it's used in a network that has been designed with stability in mind. If you just let an EIGRP network happen, without proper design considerations, however, it can easily be a nightmare to manage and to maintain. In this chapter, we discuss EIGRP network design issues, including techniques to improve your network and pitfalls to avoid. Throughout this chapter, we will build on the concepts presented in Chapter 1. We will briefly cover some fundamental questions you must consider in order to build a scalable, reliable network. We will then discuss specific design issues and suggested techniques.

Network Topology

Before we start discussing specific situations you will face when building an EIGRP network, we should start with the foundation of it all. A network that "evolves" without consideration being given to hierarchy and **address summarization** is unlikely to remain stable as it grows. Some of the strengths of EIGRP also lead to its vulnerabilities; unless you design EIGRP networks to avoid these vulnerabilities, reliability will be negatively impacted.

As the previous chapters describe, EIGRP converges extremely quickly when a change in the network occurs. This rapid convergence results from the manner in which EIGRP searches for an alternative path when the topology changes. Instead of waiting for periodic updates to advise the routing protocol of changes, EIGRP will energetically look for an alternative path if a change in the topology occurs.

When EIGRP actively pursues an alternative path to a destination, every router that could provide an alternative path is interrogated until EIGRP finds one or runs out of routers to ask. This process, known as the *query* process, is explained in detail in Chapter 1. Several techniques can reduce the number of routers involved in the query process, but almost all of those techniques require a hierarchical network topology and addressing that provides for summarization. The importance of using these techniques will be made clear later in this chapter.

Hierarchy

Typically, the **hierarchy** should reflect at least three layers: *core, distribution,* and *access,* as shown in Figure 3.1. Although the three-level hierarchy may not be appropriate for every network, it is an excellent place to start. In this model of hierarchy, the network's **core layer** comprises high-powered routers whose job is to switch packets as quickly as possible. No functions that degrade packet switching, such as access control or policy application, belong in the core of the network.

The **distribution layer** is attached to the core and uses the core to pass traffic between the access layer of the network and common access services, such as server farms and Internet access, and other locations in the distribution/access layers. The distribution layer is responsible mainly for **traffic aggregation** and route summarization. The distribution layer is also where **WAN (wide area network)** links would be connected to the core of the network.

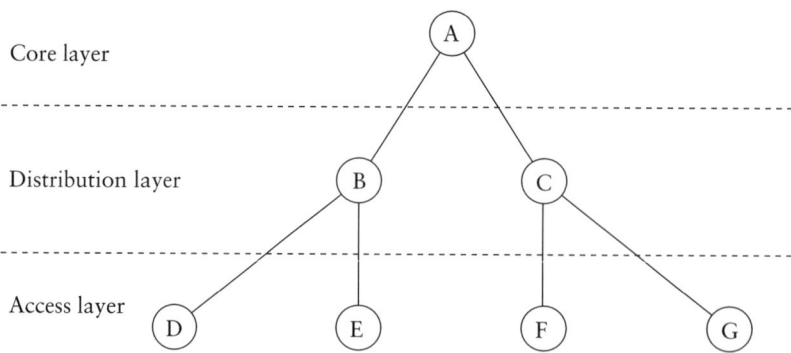

Figure 3.1 A simple hierarchical structure

The **access layer** is typically the point where users are attached to the network. Access routers are normally the least-expensive and lowest-powered routers in the network, with much lower traffic-switching performance requirements. The access layer is intended to provide access to the network to one, or at least very few, groups of users. The access layer is also where access control and policy application are performed. For example, if **quality of service** were used on the network, traffic classification and policing would most likely occur at the access layer.

Why is hierarchy important for EIGRP's stability? The well-defined roles of the various layers provide an excellent method of determining where route summarization and **information hiding** can be performed. In the next section of this chapter, we'll discuss information hiding and its importance. But remember: Without hierarchy, these extremely important tools cannot be used successfully.

Redundancy

Another aspect of the physical topology that needs to be considered is the level of **redundancy** required in order to meet the service-level requirements of the network. Redundancy is a necessary part of every network design: Failures happen, and a design that won't tolerate failure is a poor design. A network that works only when every piece of it works won't survive in the real world; redundancy must be designed into the network from the ground up.

Excessive redundancy can be worse than no redundancy at all, however. When a topology change occurs, EIGRP searches every available path—within certain limits, which we will cover later in this chapter—in order to look for an alternative, working path. When there are apparently dozens of alternative paths from a router to every destination, the amount of work required to investigate each alternative can be overwhelming. When designing a network, you should determine the level of redundancy required to provide fault-tolerant service to network users and eliminate every other path from EIGRP's list of alternatives.

One common example of excessive redundancy is two or more routers connected through numerous user segments, typically via switches and **VLANs**. The networks connecting these routers are intended to provide access for users (or to services) connected to them, rather than alternative **transit paths** through the network. By transit

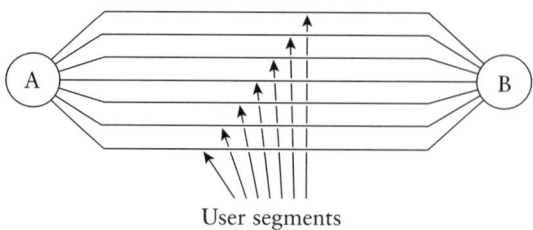

Figure 3.2 Multiple parallel user segments

traffic, we mean traffic not originating or terminating on a segment but flowing *through* the segment while traveling across the network. Figure 3.2 shows an example of excessive redundancy owing to user VLANs with routing enabled.

In order to reduce this excessive redundancy across these user segments, you should evaluate every link and determine which ones are intended to provide a routing path for transit traffic. Any segment not intended as a transit path should be removed from the EIGRP topology by applying the `passive-interface` command under the router process for each interface to be removed. For example, for the network depicted in Figure 3.2, you would configure the following:

```
router eigrp 1
passive-interface FastEthernet1.1
passive-interface FastEthernet1.2
. . .
```

The results would be the greatly simplified topology depicted in Figure 3.3.

In summary, without proper hierarchy, information hiding cannot be performed, and your EIGRP network will be susceptible to instability unnecessarily. How can you improve stability once you've created a hierarchical network with reasonable redundancy? The following sections should provide you with some insight.

Figure 3.3 Simplified topology

Minimizing Query Range

To review, if a router loses a route, such as when an interface goes down or an update is received from a neighbor withdrawing a route, or the metric to a destination has increased (become worse) and doesn't have another equal-cost path (alternative successor) or feasible successor, it sends queries to all neighbors except those connected through the interface used to reach the destination. When a router receives a query from a neighbor that was previously the successor for a given destination, and it doesn't have any alternative successors or feasible successors, the router will send its own query to its neighbors, asking them whether they know an alternative path, and so on.

In this manner, a chain of queries cascades throughout the network, stopping only when one of the following conditions is met:

- An alternative path is found.
- The end of network is reached.
- Information about the network that is the subject of the query is unknown.

In most networks of significant size, the queries may not be answered from time to time, generating Stuck in Active routes. Occasional SIAs should not be a concern, but frequent ones are. How do we minimize SIA routes? We do so by decreasing the number of routers and links involved in the query process. We call this action minimizing the **query scope** in a network. How do we minimize the query scope? Referring back to the three ways in which queries cease to be propagated, we can

- Always have unaffected alternative paths to all destinations in the network. This goal is a laudable target but hardly realistic. Remember: Excessive redundancy is bad.
- Make the end of the network happen sooner rather than later. If your network is small enough, you probably won't have SIA problems. Of course, it seems that every network is increasing in size, not decreasing, so this approach isn't a very realistic one, either.

- Make the network referenced in the query unknown. This is the answer!

If you use information hiding in order to make the paths unknown on a large part of the network, you will minimize the number of routers involved in convergence. Consequently, you will be decreasing the convergence time and, more important, the odds of getting Stuck in Active routes.

Two techniques are available that easily hide information in EIGRP networks. The flexibility of these techniques is one of the primary factors that make EIGRP a widely deployed routing protocol on large networks. By using these techniques at strategic places in the network, EIGRP will scale very well and will remain reliable in large networks. Its flexibility is far greater than that of its two primary competitors among modern routing protocols, IS-IS and OSPF. The two techniques are route summarization and **route filtering**.

First, we'll look at route summarization in an EIGRP network. Summarization for EIGRP networks has two forms. Although they are implemented quite differently, the overall impact on the query range is the same. Which technique you need to use is based on how your IP addresses are assigned.

Summarization

The first type of summarization you will encounter in EIGRP is *autosummarization*. EIGRP automatically performs summarization at major network boundaries unless you explicitly shut it off with the command no auto-summary. With autosummary enabled, any router configured with multiple network statements—routers that attach to more than one major network—will automatically send only a summary route on the major network boundary, suppressing all the network components. For example, in Figure 3.4, router A has several interfaces on the 10.0.0.0 network and several interfaces on the 172.16.0.0 network. With autosummary enabled, EIGRP will summarize all the 10.*x.x.x* components into a single route, 10.0.0.0/8, to send out all the 172.16.0.0 interfaces. Likewise, EIGRP will advertise only the 172.16.0.0/16 destination instead of the individual components through all the interfaces in the 10.0.0.0 network.

Chapter 3: EIGRP Network Design 43

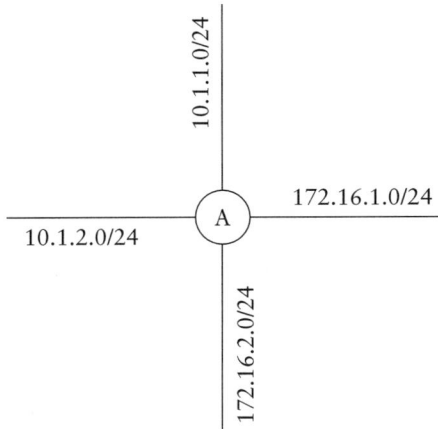

Figure 3.4 Autosummarization

Of course, this technique can be used only at major network boundaries, limiting its usefulness. Autosummary should be disabled only when **discontiguous subnets** are within your network, because discontiguous networks require the propagation of all components to all routers. A discontiguous network is one in which not all the components of a major network can be reached via links that are also part of the same major network. Although discontiguous networks are a reality, they are not a recommended design choice. See Figure 3.5 for an example of a discontiguous network.

In addition to autosummarization, EIGRP also supports manual summarization, which is much more administratively difficult but also far more flexible than autosummarization. Manual summarization lets you suppress routes and advertise a summary for those routes on any interface in the network. This flexibility permits you to do multiple lev-

Figure 3.5 A discontiguous network

els of route aggregation—difficult or impossible with IS-IS or OSPF—and allows the network's physical hierarchy to define where summarization should occur.

Remember the discussion on network hierarchy at the beginning of this chapter? A hierarchical network gives us natural points in the network to do summarization, assuming that the network addressing was also performed in a manner permitting it. In Figure 3.6, the addressing has been done with summarization in mind, allowing you to aggregate addresses on each distribution-layer router toward the core. The result of summarization is that all the destinations attached to the access routers for a single distribution router can be represented by a single route. In this case, all the destinations reachable through router B can be represented by the single route 10.1.0.0/16, and all routes reached through router C can be represented by 10.2.0.0/16.

As mentioned earlier in this chapter, the key ingredient to making EIGRP more stable and scalable is to hide information. If fewer routers have knowledge of a particular destination, fewer routers will be involved in convergence when the destination's state changes. With summarization, we are hiding the information by aggregating the component routes into one or more summary routes. Only the summary is known beyond the summarization point; the components are unknown.

Using Figure 3.6 as an example, if the interface on router D for 10.1.1.0/24 goes down, router D will send a query to router B, looking

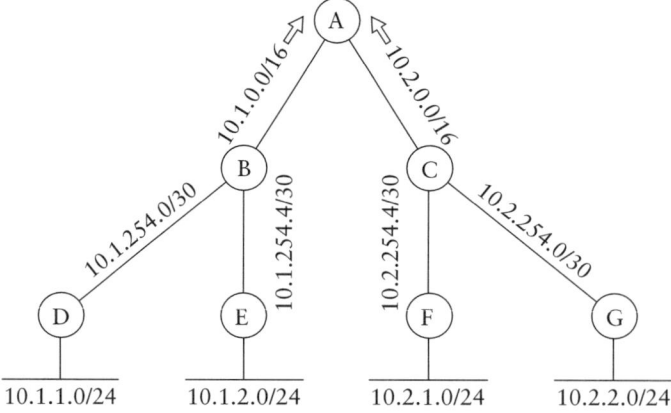

Figure 3.6 Summarization in a hierarchical network

for an alternative path. When router B receives the query, it will look in its topology table, not find an alternative path, and generate a query toward router A. When it receives the query, router A will check its topology table and will find that it also doesn't have an entry for 10.1.1.0/24 but instead has only the summary route 10.1.0.0/16. Because it doesn't have 10.1.1.0/24 in its topology table, router A will immediately send a reply to router B, reporting that it doesn't have an alternative path to 10.1.1.0/24, and the query process will be completed.

As described in Chapter 2, manual summarization is configured on each interface of a router through which a summary route should be sent. This makes the implementation of manual summarization a bit more administratively burdensome. To perform manual summarization, you must first decide where routes can be aggregated in your topology. In our example, using Figure 3.4, the job was made simple through the use of a hierarchical topology and intelligent address assignment.

Route Filtering

Filtering routes in EIGRP is another very useful technique for information hiding. In this section, we'll describe how the two techniques differ in function and will give an example of when a route filter is a better choice than summarization.

When you summarize manually or through the autosummarization process, EIGRP creates a summary route with an administrative distance of 5 with a next hop of the interface `Null0` and advertises the summary out the appropriate interfaces. All the components of the summary are filtered automatically, so only the summary is received downstream. Performing summarization creates the aggregate route and removes the components in one step.

With route filtering, on the other hand, no routes are created. The only function performed by route filtering is eliminating routes from being sent or received. Why would you want to use route filtering instead of summarization? The most common use is when the route created by the summarization causes a conflict with a real route. For example, summarizing to the **default route** (0.0.0.0/0) will create a local route to 0.0.0.0/0 through the `Null0` interface, with an administrative distance equal to 5. If a *real* default route is received by the router with the summary configured, it will be rejected because it has a worse administrative distance than the summary route created locally. The results could be disastrous!

Instead of summarizing to 0.0.0.0/0, we can filter the routes sent to the remote routers so that only the 0.0.0.0/0 route is sent. The filtering is done via the `distribute-list <number> out <interface>` command. Of course, if you decide to use this technique, you should ensure that the 0.0.0.0/0 route will always be received by the router that is filtering to just the default route.

Ensuring that 0.0.0.0/0 is always sent to the remote routers is generally done by defining what is known as a **floating static route** on the distribution-layer routers, to back up the default route learned from the exit point of the network. It wouldn't be very good if the 0.0.0.0/0 route injected for Internet access were to disappear owing to link failure or another reason, causing the *only* route used by the access router to reach all target networks, both internal and external, to disappear and to strand the users attached to access-layer routers!

To implement floating static routes, you enter the desired static route command with an administrative distance value associated with the route: `ip route 0.0.0.0 0.0.0.0 10.1.1.1 250`, for example. The administrative distance of 250 tells the router to prefer any dynamically learned route to this static one. If the dynamically derived route disappears, use the floating static route. By making the administrative distance of the static route worse than any dynamically derived route, you will use the static route in the routing table only if the dynamically derived route disappears.

Another example of route filtering as a better approach than summarization is when you want to limit the routes sent through an interface to a subset of the all known routes but don't want to limit it to only the summary. In Figure 3.7, for example, a remote site is connected to two distribution routers, one in New York and one in San Francisco. For most traffic coming from the remote sites, it doesn't matter whether the path through New York or San Francisco is used.

Summarization, however, would produce suboptimal routing. If only the 10.0.0.0/8 entry or a default route is sent from the distribution routers B and C, the remote router wouldn't know which path to take to reach the components of 10.1.0.0/16. As a result, router A could send some traffic destined to New York through router C!

Chapter 3: EIGRP Network Design 47

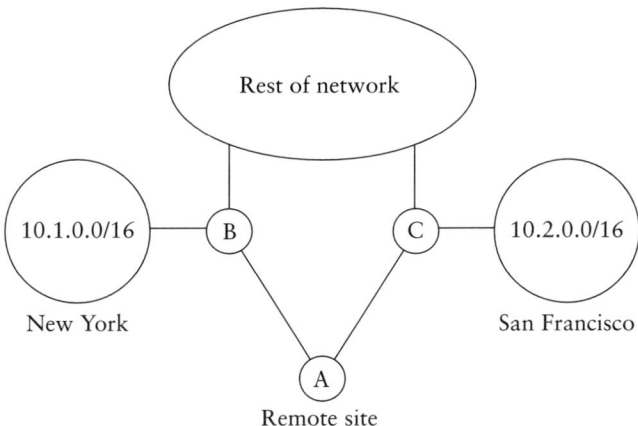

Figure 3.7 Route filtering

A more appropriate approach would be to put route filters in place, permitting only 10.0.0.0/8 and the subnets located in New York to be advertised from router B and only 10.0.0.0/8 and subnets located in San Francisco to be advertised by router C. Of course, if the 10.0.0.0/8 route doesn't exist in the network, you must define a local static route—typically to `null0`—and redistribute it into EIGRP. You would probably want to filter this redistributed static route to prevent other distribution-layer routers from learning about it.

Stub Routers

Defining a router as a *stub* means that it is used only to attach user segments to the remainder of the network via one or more paths. Figure 3.8 gives an example of a situation in which defining a router as a stub is useful.

In Figure 3.8, three access sites, D, E, and G, are connected to the distribution layer via two serial links each. These sites, known as **dual-homed remotes,** are intended to provide reliable access to the remainder of the network for the users located at the remote sites. Although the dual legs could provide an alternative path for traffic from the distribution layer through the remote and back to the distribution layer, this behavior isn't what was intended. Configuring each of these remote routers as stubs tells EIGRP that they are not intended to be a transit path for network traffic traveling from one distribution router to another.

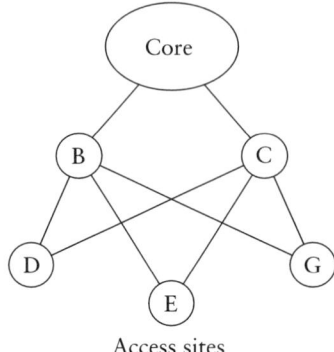

Figure 3.8 Stub networks

When the remote router is defined as a stub, it will advertise only local routes: connected, static, or summary. This means that any route learned from one distribution-layer router will not be advertised back out to the other distribution-layer router. We can provide this function with distribution lists, but defining the router as a stub router automatically causes this route filtering to happen.

Additionally, and more important, when a router is defined as a stub router, the distribution-layer routers know that they will never find an alternative path through the stub router and thus will never even send queries toward the remotes. This is a major advantage because it now removes all the stub routers from the query process entirely. The distribution lists mentioned earlier block updates but not queries; if the remote routers are not defined as stubs, queries will continue to flow to them.

Multiple Autonomous Systems

Some network administrators decrease the query scope by defining multiple autonomous systems and redistributing among them. Although this approach may make EIGRP vaguely resemble OSPF with its area hierarchy, it doesn't contain the query scope as expected. When a query reaches the end of an autonomous system, a reply to the query is indeed sent back. Unless summarization or route filters are implemented, however, a new query will then start up in the next autonomous system. It's as if the query were given new life!

Some network administrators have successfully implemented multiple autonomous systems with the heavy use of route filtering and summarization. Given political or administrative reasons to make different portions of the network different autonomous systems, it may be a good way to implement this separation. However, it isn't helping to minimize the query scope.

Multiple Routing Protocols

Query scope can also be decreased by removing from the EIGRP topology links and routers that don't need to be running EIGRP! For example, if an access site has a single path into the rest of the network and the link to the site is of poor quality, you should consider removing it from EIGRP. Configure a static default route on the remote router to provide a path for the traffic from the remote, and configure a static at the distribution-layer router that provides a path to the destinations at the remote. Redistribute the static routes at the distribution-layer router into EIGRP so the rest of the network has the information it needs to reach the remote destinations. This is a drastic measure but is sometimes the best approach to take.

Another approach gaining in popularity is to use **ODR (on-demand routing)** to get the routes from the access sites into the distribution layer and then to redistribute those ODR routes into EIGRP. ODR routing takes advantage of the **CDP (Cisco Discovery Protocol)**, which advertises the interface addresses of each router to its directly connected neighbors. The addresses advertised are limited, however, to the primary interface addresses. If a router has static routes, secondary addresses, or any other source of routes, ODR will not propagate them.

In summary, numerous tools and techniques are available for decreasing the query scope of an EIGRP network. It is vitally important for you to evaluate the various methods of containing the convergence process to the area of the network where it is necessary. Evaluate each of these techniques and choose the ones that make the most sense in your network. If your addressing will not permit summarization and your topology is nonhierarchical, you may need to consider changing some of the basic structure of your network. If you don't make wise choices in your topology and addressing, you will be fighting an uphill battle. If you don't use the information-hiding techniques available to you, your network stability will be in jeopardy.

Path Selection Issues

In this section, we discuss various aspects of path selection in EIGRP networks. (See Chapter 1 for an explanation of the metric components.) Here, we'll deal with design issues associated with changing metric parameters (bandwidth and delay) on an interface, changing the *K value, variance,* asymmetrical routing, and default routing strategies. We will start by discussing modifying interface metric parameters to influence the path EIGRP chooses to a given destination.

Changing the Metric Components on an Interface

Sometimes, you'll want to change the next hop chosen through the normal metric calculation/path selection process in EIGRP. If the next hop for some but not all destinations through a particular path need to be influenced, it's best to use route maps to influence only those routes rather than changing interface information, which influences the path chosen for all destinations.

If all the routes through a particular next hop need to be influenced, however, the natural method of modifying the path selection is to change one of the components used in the metric calculation to make the routes more or less desirable. The choice then becomes which parameter should be changed. As explained in Chapter 1, normally only two parameters are used in the metric: bandwidth and delay. Because both bandwidth and delay can be modified on a single interface, which should you change to modify path selection?

Let's take it one parameter at a time. What is typically called the bandwidth parameter in the metric is the *minimum* bandwidth in the path to the target network. On the router doing the metric calculation, the smallest bandwidth between it and the target of the route is included in the bandwidth portion of the metric calculation. By modifying the bandwidth parameter on an interface, you may or may not be changing the metric for a particular route!

Chapter 3: EIGRP Network Design

In Figure 3.9, the minimum bandwidth to network 10.1.2.0/24, from router A's point of view, is the T1 (1.544 Mbps) between it and router B. If you decreased this bandwidth value to 512Kbps in order to influence path selection, the metric for 10.1.2.0/24 would indeed change. However, the minimum bandwidth to network 10.1.4.0/24 is 128K, the lowest-speed link to 10.1.4.0/24 from router A. So the change made between router A and router B in order to influence path selection had absolutely no impact on the metric for the route to 10.1.4.0/24!

EIGRP also uses the bandwidth configured on an interface to determine the **pacing interval** between EIGRP packets. If you change the bandwidth parameter to influence path selection, you may be changing pacing intervals to such an extent that the convergence of the network will be put in jeopardy!

For example, if you changed the bandwidth statement on an interface to be 1Kbps, in order to make a path a backup route—normally not preferred in EIGRP's routing decisions—you would inadvertently leave EIGRP with only 0.5Kbps to send all its updates, queries, and replies! This bandwidth is probably not enough to even have the neighbor relationship between routers successfully be established! Obviously, changing the bandwidth value can have consequences far beyond those intended.

Delay is the other parameter you can use in order to influence path selection. Table 3.1 lists some of the default delay values for each interface type. These default values can also be overridden on each interface, using the `delay` command. The delay values are cumulative, so from a router doing the metric calculation, all delays between it and the target network are added to arrive at the delay value in the metric. The delay on the outbound interface of the router toward the target is included.

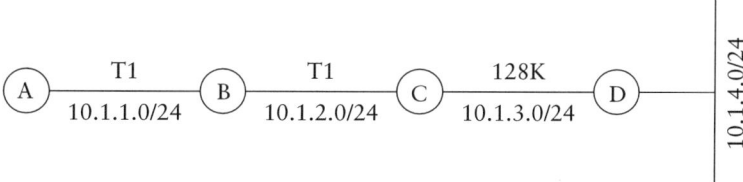

Figure 3.9 The effect of changing the minimum bandwidth

Table 3.1. Default Delays by Interface Type

Interface Type	Delay (Microseconds)
TAXI	10
SONET	8
E3	20
DS3	19
ISDN PRI and Serial	2,000
Fast Ethernet	10
Ethernet	100
FDDI	10
Tunnel	50,000

Because the delays for each link are added to arrive at a total, modifying the delay value on a link will almost certainly change the metric of all destinations reachable across this link. It is possible, although unlikely, to set the delay value high enough so that a minor change to the delay will not change the overall, or composite, metrics. This behavior is possible because of the way the delay value is stored internally. The display of the delay value on the interface is in microseconds, and the command is entered in tens of microseconds. Therefore, if the value shown by show interface is 20,000 and you want to increase the delay to 25,000, the interface configuration command would be delay 2500.

Offset Lists

Path selection can also be impacted with the offset-list command, which you can use to tell EIGRP to add extra delay to updates received from or delivered to a particular neighbor. Furthermore, the **offset list** can be used with an access list to define a subset of routes to apply the additional delay to. In this manner, you can easily select which routes will be influenced by the command.

For example, if you wanted router A in Figure 3.10 to prefer the path through router C for packets destined to network 10.1.4.0/24 but

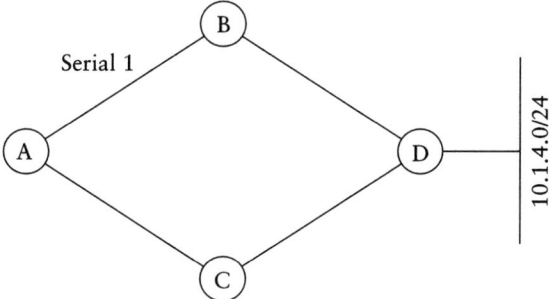

Figure 3.10 Offset lists

would prefer the remainder of the destinations go through router B, you would use the following offset list to accomplish the purpose:

```
hostname A
!
router eigrp 100
  offset-list 10 in 100 serial 1
!
access-list 10 permit 10.1.4.0 0.0.0.0
```

Changing *K* Values

One additional tool that can be used to influence path selection in an EIGRP network is to change the K values used to determine the weight of each element in the total metric calculation. The K values can be changed so that EIGRP uses additional elements, such as the reliability of a link, in the metric calculation. Also, the K values can be changed so that EIGRP acts more like RIP, treating the delay as a hop count through the network.

It's often tempting to use some of the other metric attributes that EIGRP includes in its metric calculation beyond the defaults (minimum bandwidth and total delay), but before embarking on this course, you need to understand the significant limitations. The additional parameters that can theoretically be used to determine path selection include load, reliability, and the minimum MTU along the path.

At first glance, using load or reliability to determine which path should be used seems a reasonable—even desirable—design idea. For example, if a particular path is congested (load is high) or having physical-layer errors (reliability is low), it would be nice if the routing protocol would avoid using it. To accomplish this dynamic rerouting around poor or overloaded links, you might want to change the K values so the load and reliability compute into the metric. But although this change may be logical, it's not useful.

Unlike IGRP, which sends periodic updates and can also use reliability and load in the metric calculation, EIGRP sends updates to its neighbors only when the topology changes. Unfortunately, a change in load or reliability isn't considered a topology change, so a change in either load or reliability will not cause an update to be sent. This makes enabling the K values for load or reliability relatively useless.

For example, the load on a link could increase dramatically, yet a router running EIGRP will not notify any of its neighbors of the changed load value even if the K value for load is enabled. If an update is sent owing to a topology change, the higher load will be reflected in the update, so the neighbors would then learn about the busy link.

Of course, if traffic is diverted owing to the metric change with the high load and the load drops significantly, again a router running EIGRP will not notify any of its neighbors of the change. A fairly underutilized link will continue to be avoided, based on the state of the link when the last update occurred, not the current state of the link. Only on the next topology change causing an update would neighbors learn of the new conditions of the link.

So, changing the K values to pay attention to load or reliability of a link is not very useful. What about the other changes some people make to the K values? Sometimes, you might want to minimize the number of router hops taken to any destination and thus want to change EIGRP's behavior to more closely resemble RIP's normal behavior. In other words, you may want to base routing decisions on hop count instead of the lowest metric calculated from the minimum bandwidth and total delay. How can you do this? If you eliminate the K value for bandwidth and manually define all the delay values so they are the same on all interfaces of all routers in the network, you will end up with a hop count–based routing protocol.

Variance

Variance changes the path selection process by permitting routes with unequal costs to be installed in the routing table, thus allowing the router to load share over multiple unequal-cost paths in proportion to their metrics. Normally, EIGRP and all routing protocols will default to installing up to four equal-cost paths in the routing table. With variance, EIGRP goes beyond equal-cost paths and permits unequal-cost paths to be installed. Even so, EIGRP still guarantees that each route installed in the routing table will be loop free by allowing only *feasible successors* to be installed.

Figure 3.11 shows two paths from router A to network 10.1.1.0/24. The link from router A through router B is significantly better than the path from router A through router C and will be, by default, the only route installed in A's routing table, leaving the path through router C idle. Because you probably don't want to see links you are paying for idle, you can use variance to change the default behavior of installing only the best route in the routing table.

By adding the command variance 2 under the router EIGRP process, EIGRP will use the variance value as a multiplier to the best metric—feasible distance through the current successor—to determine which other routes should also be included in the routing table. In the network in Figure 3.11, router A's metric for network 10.1.1.0/24 through router B is 6,500, and through router C is 10,000. With the variance set to 2, EIGRP will multiply the route through router B by 2 and then compare it to the metric through router C. Because the cost of

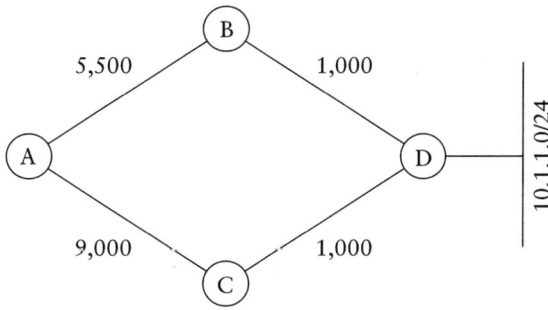

Figure 3.11 Variance across unequal-cost paths

the path through router C is lower than the cost of the path through router B, owing to the multiplier, the path through router C is also installed in the routing table.

You might think that using variance could cause congestion problems on the link between router A and router C, as we've made the path through router C appear equal to the path through router B, which is, in fact, a better route. Couldn't this cause more traffic to use this path than it can handle? EIGRP is smart enough to realize that the variance statement didn't change the capacity of the links and will send traffic from router A to router C path proportional to the variance. In other words, traffic will be apportioned to the links, based on the metrics toward the destination.

As not too much traffic will be sent over the lower-bandwidth link, it sounds like a fine plan. Can any alternative path be used to load share with the variance command? No. The alternative path must also meet the feasibility condition, which was explained in Chapter 1. It's logical that you shouldn't use an alternative path to load share if it may introduce a routing loop. By meeting the feasibility condition, the loop-free nature of the alternative path is ensured.

Does using variance have any drawbacks? Unfortunately, the answer is yes. You must keep two issues in mind before deciding to use variance in your network: its global scope and the possibility of packets arriving out of order.

In the preceding example, variance was used to solve a single problem—using all the available bandwidth from router A to network 10.1.1.0/24. By configuring variance, this problem was solved. What isn't so obvious, however, is that the variance multiplier is now used on *all* routes in the topology table. Even if a single destination is the desired target of the change, the impact to other routes could also be felt, whether desired or not. It is impossible to limit the scope of variance.

The second possible problem introduced by the use of variance is the very real possibility of out-of-order packets. Some IP stacks are more tolerant than others about receiving out-of-order packets; the overhead involved in reordering out-of-order packets may be significant in some cases. In fact, it's possible that the performance lost through reordering out-of-order packets at the end systems more than negates any gains realized through the load sharing across the less desirable link.

Most modern stacks should tolerate out-of-order packets fairly well, but you should be aware of the possibility of creating additional work for the end systems before deciding on variance as a tool to use. Beyond this, some switching modes within a Cisco router will produce very few out-of-order packets even when variance is configured, such as fast switching and **CEE (Cisco Express Forwarding)**. One other consideration when attempting to load share across links—whether they are equal cost or unequal cost—is that the type of switching used on the router will greatly affect how much load sharing you can achieve, such as which fast-switching routes are cached on a per destination basis. If most of the traffic has only one destination, most of the traffic will end up traversing one link at a time, regardless of how many equal-cost paths exist.

Asymmetric Routing

Asymmetric routing means that the path between two particular hosts on a network may be different in each direction. You may think that the routers are acting incorrectly, but in reality, they are acting as expected. In the following example, we will demonstrate this principle.

In Figure 3.12, host X sends router A packets destined to host Y on network 10.1.1.0/24. When it receives a packet, router A will evaluate the alternative paths in its routing table to reach host Y. Because it has only a single path to reach 10.1.1.0/24, router A forwards the packet on to router B, which then evaluates its paths to reach 10.1.1.0/24. From router B's viewpoint, the best metric to reach 10.1.1.0/24 is through router C, because the minimum bandwidth to reach 10.1.1.0/24 is 1.544Mbps, but the minimum bandwidth is 512Kbps through router D.

On the return path, router E sees two equal-cost paths to reach host X because the 128Kbps link between router A and router B is the minimum bandwidth for both paths back to host X through both router D and router C. Because the delay values are the same on each interface—delay for a serial link defaults to 20,000—both paths appear to have equal metrics, and router E load shares between them.

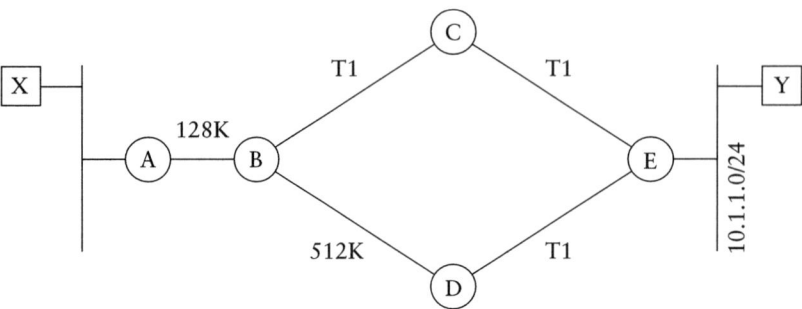

Figure 3.12 Asymmetric routing

As this example shows, the path chosen in each direction is independent. You shouldn't count on the path to a target being reflected in the return path.

Default Routing Strategy

If, where, and how to originate the default route for the network also needs to be thought out when considering path selection through the network. A default route is used to provide a path for a router to send packets to if the destination address of the packet is unknown and is often used to provide a routing path to external destinations, such as the Internet, and for hiding information.

The most common reason for propagating a default route throughout your network is to provide a path to external destinations. For instance, it isn't necessary to carry the entire Internet routing table into EIGRP or any other interior gateway protocol when probably only one or two carefully controlled points will exit out of your network toward the Internet. Instead, it makes more sense to carry one route, a default route.

This strategy also carries an element of the second reason for using a default route: information hiding. You can go further than hiding the Internet's routing table from routers in your network with a default route, though. For example, in Figure 3.13, router B doesn't need to know about every possible remote site reachable through router C.

Router B needs to know only that if it doesn't know how to reach a destination, it can simply forward the traffic on to router A. This is a perfect design in which to use a default route to reduce the amount of

Chapter 3: EIGRP Network Design

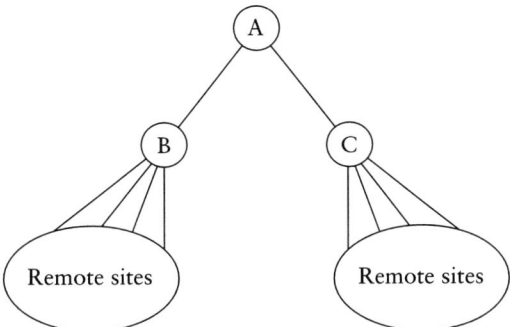

Figure 3.13 Hiding information with default routes

information routers B and C and the routers behind them must work with when a topology change occurs.

Once you've decided to use a default route, what are your alternatives for generating and propagating it? You can use two strategies, each with many variations. The first alternative is to use a `default network` statement at one or many places in the network. The second alternative is to use a true default route (0.0.0.0/0).

The Default Network: The **default network** is an approach left over from the IGRP days. IGRP had no way to represent the default route (0.0.0.0/0) in the IGRP packet, so an alternative strategy had to be created. The method Cisco selected was to allow you to create a default network via the global command `ip default-network <address>`. The destination address defined using the `ip default-network` command is flagged in the IGRP and EIGRP updates as a *candidate default route*.

When it receives a route marked as a candidate default, a router flags it in the routing table: Look for a * beside the route. The best candidate default route is chosen as the default network, and the next hop toward the default network is chosen as the gateway of last resort. All this information can be seen by using the command `show ip route`.

```
router>show ip route
Codes: C - connected, S - static, I - IGRP, R - RIP,
  M - mobile, B - BGP
```

```
        D - EIGRP, EX - EIGRP external, O - OSPF, IA - OSPF
          inter area
        N1 - OSPF NSSA external type 1, N2 - OSPF NSSA
          external type 2
        E1 - OSPF external type 1, E2 - OSPF external type 2,
          E - EGP
        i - IS-IS, L1 - IS-IS level-1, L2 - IS-IS level-2,
          * - candidate default
        U - per-user static route, o - ODR

Gateway of last resort is 10.1.50.8 to network 192.168.20.0

     10.0.0.0/24 is subnetted, 1 subnets
C       10.1.50.0 is directly connected, Serial0
C       10.1.14.0 is directly connected, Ethernet0
E*      192.168.20.0 via 10.1.50.8
```

Although this method of default routing is not necessarily intuitive, it works pretty well.

The Default Route: The default route is another name for the route with all zeros in its address and mask—an address of 0.0.0.0 and a prefix length of 0. This route is typically introduced by a static route defined as

```
ip route 0.0.0.0 0.0.0.0 [<next-hop>|<interface>]
```

This static route is then redistributed into EIGRP, using the command

```
router eigrp 100
 redistribute static
 default-metric 10000 10 1 255 1500
```

Remember that IGRP is not capable of representing a default route in its update packets, so IGRP cannot propagate a default route learned from a static route or other source. EIGRP doesn't have this restriction, however. In our example in Figure 3.13, the natural place to put a static default route is router A. Router A would then distribute a default route so the rest of the network would use the path to it as the way to reach any destination address not in the routing table.

One word of caution, however: in earlier versions of Cisco IOS, Cisco routers defaulted to classful routing. While routing in a classful

Chapter 3: EIGRP Network Design

environment, a router assumes that knowledge of one subnet within a major network implies knowledge of every subnet within a major network. To see why this is a problem, look at Figure 3.14.

Let's assume that both routers B and C are configured for classful routing and that router A is passing only a default route out to them (0.0.0.0/0). If it receives a packet destined to 10.2.1.1, router B will examine its routing table and find that it knows about some parts of the 10.0.0.0/8 network (components of 10.1.0.0/16) but not this destination in particular.

Router B will assume that 10.2.1.1 does not exist and will drop the packet. If it is configured for classless routing, using the `ip classless` command, router B will ignore the classful routing rules and will forward the packet along its default route (or best supernet), toward router A.

Default Network or Default Route? Which strategy should you use: default network or default route? If you are still running any IGRP in your network, you must use the default-network strategy. It wouldn't work very well to use a default route, then lose the ability to propagate this default anywhere in the network running IGRP.

Because you can define the default network on multiple routers in the network when using a default network, you aren't reliant on a single or a few default origination points. The disadvantage of using the default-network approach is that it takes time to converge on a change in the path to the default network. A process that looks for changes in the gateway of

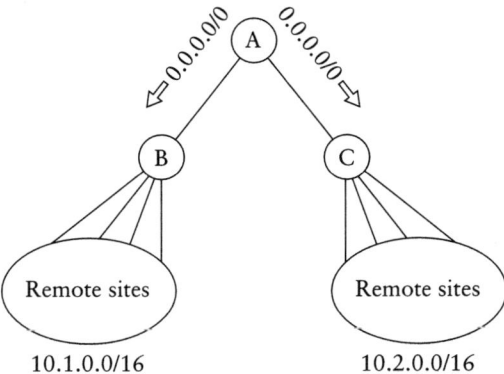

Figure 3.14 Classful routing

last resort runs every minute, so it may take up to a minute to reconverge on a new default network once the topology has changed.

With the default route, the convergence on a change in the path to the default route will be as fast as any other EIGRP route. It can be significantly faster than convergence using the default network. A disadvantage of using the default route is that it is difficult to inject it in multiple places in the network, so the network is reliant on maintaining a path to the point where the static is redistributed into the network.

WAN and Dial Issues

We're now going to change directions a little by focusing on some specific areas you need to consider in order to build and maintain a stable EIGRP network. One of the more troublesome parts of most networks is the *wide area network (WAN)* links. These links typically have low bandwidths and low reliability and are the cause of many instability problems in EIGRP. In this section, we will discuss several considerations for WAN links and strategies that will increase the EIGRP stability across these links.

Frame Relay and Bandwidth Statements

One potential problem EIGRP may face with frame relay links is that the rate at which the router connects to the link is not necessarily the rate at which EIGRP can reliably deliver packets. In Figure 3.15, for example, the **access rate** for the connection to the frame relay network

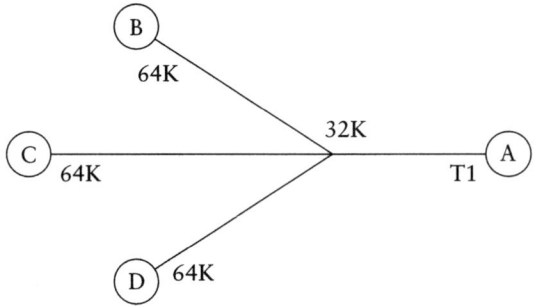

Figure 3.15 A hub-and-spoke network

on router A is T1 (1.544Mbps), but the access rate from router B is 64Kbps. Additionally, frame relay service providers may provide a **CIR (committed information rate),** for each connection, defining the data rate the provider will guarantee to deliver across the link. Any traffic that exceeds the CIR value is subject to being discarded in the frame relay network. In Figure 3.15, the CIR for our example link is 32Kbps.

Why should EIGRP care about the available delivery rate on the link? If it is sending updates, queries, or replies across a link, EIGRP should reasonably expect that the traffic it is sending will be delivered to the remote end. Because routers normally try to send data on a link as quickly as the physical link will accept it, EIGRP's packets would leave router A at 1.544Mbps into the frame relay cloud. Even if the traffic made it across the frame relay network at this rate, it can be delivered to router B only at 64Kbps. However, because the CIR is only half that rate, much of the traffic would probably be discarded in the cloud, anyway!

As EIGRP is most likely going to be sending large amounts of updates, queries, or replies during times of network instability, the worst thing to happen would be if the packets used to converge on the network changes are themselves being dropped. Regaining network stability would definitely be in jeopardy.

In order to avoid this problem, EIGRP uses the defined bandwidth value to determine how quickly it could send EIGRP traffic to its neighbors. The bandwidth value on the interface is now used to define the pacing interval EIGRP will use to put gaps between packets to ensure that it will not overwhelm the intervening network. By default, EIGRP will not use more than 50 percent of the defined bandwidth for reliable packets (updates, queries, and replies). This percentage can be changed on a per interface basis, using the command `ip eigrp <AS> bandwidth-percentage <percent>`. Later in this section, we will explain why it may be desirable to change the bandwidth percentage.

For this pacing improvement to work, however, you must manually define the bandwidth values on each frame relay interface/subinterface. Although it seems to be laborious, it is necessary to make EIGRP behave correctly on frame relay networks. The results are worth the effort! In most of the following discussion, we refer to frame relay networks, but the principles also apply to other technologies, such as **SMDS (switched** multimegabit data service), ATM (asynchronous transfer mode), and ISDN/PRI (integrated services digital network/primary rate interface).

Frame relay networks have primarily two scenarios, and each has its own requirements for defining the bandwidth. These two scenarios also have some variations, but the principles are the same. In the next section we will discuss the differences in defining bandwidth in **point-to-point subinterfaces** and multipoint interfaces/subinterfaces.

Point-to-Point Subinterfaces

With point-to-point subinterfaces, it's very simple to determine how to implement the bandwidth statement correctly. Each point-to-point subinterface should have the bandwidth set to the CIR value of the **PVC (permanent virtual circuit)—DLCI (data link connection identifier)—** mapped to the subinterface. If the frame relay PVC has 0 CIR, the bandwidth should be set to something less than the lowest access rate of either end of the PVC. In other words, the bandwidth should be set to a value that describes the data rate EIGRP should reasonably expect will be available for it to use. As mentioned earlier, EIGRP will use no more than 50 percent of this bandwidth value for its reliable packets.

Oversubscribed networks will require you to modify this approach slightly. If the total of all the CIR values exceeds the access rate at the hub of a hub-and-spoke network and if you set the bandwidth to the CIR for each subinterface, EIGRP will believe, falsely, that it has more bandwidth available than it truly has. In other words, do not let the aggregate bandwidth value of all subinterfaces combined on an interface exceed the access rate of the interface.

Sometimes, for network management performance reports to be correct, the bandwidth value may need to reflect the CIR value for each subinterface instead of the decreased value set owing to oversubscription, as mentioned previously. If the aggregate bandwidth values exceed the access rate in this case, you should use the `ip eigrp <AS> bandwidth-percentage <percent>` statement, as described in Chapter 2, to tell EIGRP to use less than 50 percent of the defined bandwidth.

Multipoint Interfaces and Subinterfaces

For multipoint interfaces/subinterfaces, determining the correct bandwidth value to define is a little more complicated. With the point-to-point

Chapter 3: EIGRP Network Design

subinterfaces described earlier, each subinterface connects to only one neighbor; therefore, the defined bandwidth should reflect whatever data rate one can expect to deliver to the neighbor reachable over the subinterface. On multipoint frame relay interfaces/subinterfaces, however, this is not the case.

By definition, a multipoint frame relay interface/subinterface can have many PVCs connecting to many neighbors, all reachable through the same interface or subinterface. The main interface is always a multipoint interface. Because numerous neighbors are normally reachable through the multipoint interface, EIGRP does not use just the defined bandwidth to determine the pacing interface for each neighbor but instead divides the bandwidth value by the number of neighbors to determine the pacing interval for each neighbor.

For example, if the network in Figure 3.15 is using a multipoint subinterface from router A to the four remote routers instead of the point-to-point subinterfaces described earlier, the bandwidth value on the frame relay interface would have to change. EIGRP would look at the defined bandwidth on router A's frame relay interface and divide it by 3, and then take 50 percent of the resulting value as the maximum amount of EIGRP traffic it can send to any one neighbor. Therefore, when defining the bandwidth value on a multipoint interface/subinterface, you should multiply the CIR values for the remote routers by the number of neighbors in order to determine the bandwidth value.

But what if the remotes have significantly different CIRs? If the PVC from router A to router C had a CIR value of 512Kbps and the other two have CIR values of 64Kbps, what value would you use at the hub? In this case, you multiply the *lowest* CIR value by the number of neighbors to reach the proper bandwidth value. Although it may constrict the EIGRP packet delivery unnecessarily to the higher-CIR neighbor, it will at least ensure that the lower-CIR neighbors will not be overwhelmed.

An even better idea for multipoint interface with highly disparate CIR rates for neighbors is to split the interface into multiple subinterfaces. In our example, the 512Kbps CIR neighbor could be put on its own point-to-point subinterface, and the bandwidth for the remaining two neighbors could then be properly defined to reflect the expected date rate.

So far, our context has been frame relay interfaces, but the principles also apply to other pseudoshared networks, such as ATM and SMDS interfaces. Similar to frame relay, ATM can have multipoint and point-to-point subinterfaces, and the same pacing requirements exist if the bandwidth is T1 or less. If the bandwidth is greater than T1, the pacing function is turned off.

With SMDS interfaces, another problem we often encounter is that sites connecting to the SMDS cloud may have vastly different access rates, resulting in conditions similar to the ones you might find on a hub-and-spoke frame relay network. Sites with very high access rates into the network can easily overwhelm sites with much lower access rates.

ISDN PRI interfaces using dialer groups or dialer lists also present significant challenges for configuring interface bandwidths. In this case, each ISDN **BRI (basic rate interface)** dialed in becomes a neighbor on a shared network, which appears to EIGRP as a multipoint interface. So, can we just apply the techniques defined earlier for multipoint interfaces to PRIs? Unfortunately, the answer is no.

With frame relay multipoint interfaces, you have a very good idea of how many neighbors you can expect to see through the multipoint interface. With an ISDN PRI, this isn't the case. One neighbor could be dialed in, which would mean that a bandwidth value of 64Kbps would be appropriate, or 24 neighbors could be dialed in, which would require a bandwidth value of 1.544Mbps. A dialer group could span multiple PRIs and could have 24, 48, or even more neighbors dialing into a single dialer interface! What a quandary!

The two approaches to resolving this issue are (1) don't use dialer interfaces or (2) make the bandwidth setting unimportant. Instead of using dialer groups, you can use dialer profiles, so each remote site dialing in is verified by **PAP/CHAP** and then associated with a virtual interface based on its identity. The bandwidth statement will be applied against each profile, not against the entire dialer group. Virtual templates can also be used in the same manner.

The second approach is to make the bandwidth value less of a factor by filtering the routes sent across the link to such an extent that any bandwidth available is enough to support it! Typically, the filtering is done via a `summary-address` statement or `distribute-list`, so that only a default route or one or more major network routes are allowed

Chapter 3: EIGRP Network Design

across the link. By permitting a very few update packets to be sent across the link, the amount of bandwidth available to move it is not as significant a problem. Since dialup connections—even via ISDN—are very limited in their bandwidth, limiting the amount of routing updates across the link is a good approach in any case.

Dual-Homed Remotes

Another issue you will need to consider when designing a network is minimizing the complexity by eliminating the reflection of routes through dual-homed remotes. In many networks, remote sites are connected via two frame relay PVCs—or other technology, but frame relay is the most prevalent—to the distribution layer. Figure 3.16 shows an example of dual-homed remote connection between remotes (routers C, D, and E) and the distribution routers (routers A and B).

Typically, the remote routers are given two PVCs to provide resiliency in the event of a PVC or router failure. The reason for two links to router C and the other remotes is so EIGRP can circumvent a failure of router A, router B, or either of the two PVCs connecting them to router C. Additionally, the two PVCs may be provided for load sharing of traffic from each remote site back to the distribution layer.

What is typically *not* intended for these two links is to use the remote routers (C, D, and E) for transit traffic. For example, traffic at the distribution layer can be routed from router A to router C and then back down the other leg to router B for delivery elsewhere. Although it

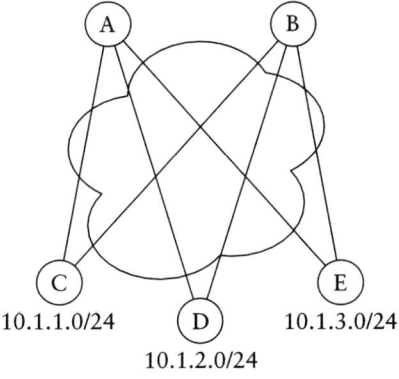

Figure 3.16 Dual-homed remotes

is possible, it is most likely not desirable or intended. Unfortunately, EIGRP has no idea what you intended; instead, it sees only what paths are possible and takes all of them into consideration when routing convergence is required.

This result exhibits itself when a routing update is sent from router A to router C; router C will turn around and readvertise the route back to router B. Likewise, when an update is received on router C from router B, router C will be a good neighbor and send it on to router A. If you look in the topology table on router A and router B, using the command `show ip eigrp topology all-links`, you will see topology table entries for each target network through every one of the remote sites!

Although EIGRP doesn't have a problem sorting out the correct path, all of the unused, undesired alternatives must be taken into account in the convergence process when there is a topology change. This process can become time-consuming and ugly. Two general strategies can rectify this situation:

- Limiting through ignorance what is known on the remote
- Filtering the reflection itself

In the first case, you can put `summary-address` statements or `distribute-lists` on the distribution routers so the remote routers aren't receiving the component routes to reflect. The remote routers would then reflect only the summary or limited route set permitted by the `distribute-list`, decreasing the complexity for the majority of the routes in the network.

The second method is a little more administratively tiresome but is probably the better method for retaining full functionality on the remote routers and limiting the reflection of routes. On each remote, a distribution list would be defined, limiting its routing advertisements on the WAN links to include only the routes that are local to the remote site. In other words, define which subnets must be advertised by a remote router to provide reachability to the resources at the remote site, and permit only these subnets in the routing updates. This is done by a `distribute-list` out globally or per interface and stops the advertisement of any routes learned from one distribution router from being reflected to the other distribution router.

Chapter 3: EIGRP Network Design

As an example, let's return to Figure 3.16, which shows several remote routers with their dual-homed connections. In order to keep router C from reflecting the routes learned from router A, such as 10.1.1.0/24, 10.1.2.0/24, and so on, back to router B, router C would put in the following command:

```
router eigrp 1
 distribute-list 1 out
!
access-list 1 permit 10.1.1.0 0.0.0.255
```

This means that router C will be allowed to advertise only routes beginning with 10.1.1.0, which will stop it from advertising routes from one distribution router to another.

Another approach to providing service to dual-homed remotes is to use EIGRP stub network support. With stub networks, the remote router would be able to advertise only connected, static, or locally originated summary routes toward the distribution routers. This approach will automatically stop the remote router from reflecting routes from one distribution router to the other.

A third approach to supporting dual-homed remotes is the use of CDP-based *on-demand routing (ODR)* for getting the remote subnets into the distribution routers, then redistributing these ODR routes into EIGRP at the distribution layer. One limitation with this approach is that ODR will advertise only directly connected primary interfaces. If secondary addresses are defined or if redistributed or dynamically derived routes from the remote site need to be advertised, this approach will not work.

Low-Speed NBMA Links and SIAs

Another situation to avoid arises from the relationship between low-speed **NBMA (nonbroadcast multiaccess)** networks and SIA routes. As described in Chapter 1, SIA routes occur when a route goes active, one or more queries are issued trying to find an alternative path, and not all replies are received. How do low-speed NBMA networks play a part in this situation?

First, what is an NBMA network? As the name implies, an NBMA network supports access from multiple routers at the same time but doesn't support broadcast packets. For example, frame relay multipoint networks allow a single IP subnet to be shared by multiple routers in a partial or full mesh topology. Although each router shares an IP subnet with the other routers across the frame relay cloud, they cannot send a single broadcast packet and have it simultaneously delivered to all the other routers on that subnet. Instead, the pseudobroadcast packets would need to be replicated and sent to each neighbor independently.

The challenge in using a low-speed NBMA network involves the timing of retransmission timeouts. As explained in Chapter 1, the default hold time for high-speed, point-to-point, or broadcast-based media is 15 seconds, or three times the **hello interval** of 5 seconds. For low-speed NBMA networks, such as frame relay multipoint, X.25, and SMDS, the default hold time is 180 seconds, which is three times the hello interval of 60 seconds. This 3-minute hold timer can create a problem in a network because it is the same value as the SIA timer.

Figure 3.17 shows an example of a network containing a low-speed (T1 or less) NBMA network (frame relay multipoint). When the Ethernet on router A fails, router A sends a query to its neighbors, looking for an alternative path to reach 10.1.1.0/24. In our example, assume that we are also having a problem with packet delivery to router D, which is a remote site on a multipoint frame relay link.

Router C will continue to retransmit reliable packets to router D 16 times *and* then wait until the hold time period has expired. In other words, router C will send the same updates over and over again, for 3 minutes. Then router C will declare router D down, owing to retransmit limit exceeded. In the meantime, however, the query originated from router A would be queued behind the update packets in router C and not complete before the 3-minute period has expired. Because it

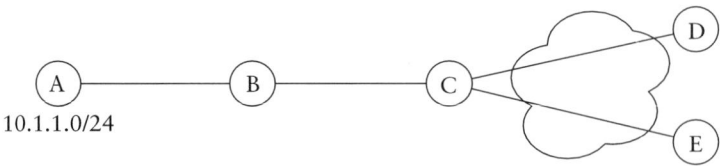

Figure 3.17 Low-speed links and SIAs

takes 3 minutes to declare the neighbor down, router A can be waiting those same 3 minutes for the replies to its queries. Thus, router A's SIA timer will also expire, and the neighbor relationship between routers A and B will be reset.

If the link between routers C and D were to have a lower hold time, the neighbor relationship between them would have been declared down prior to the SIA timer expiration on router A. When it reinitializes router D, owing to the retransmit limit exceeded, router C will send the infinity reply back to router B, saying that it doesn't have an alternative path to 10.1.1.0/24. Router C terminates the active condition, assuming that all other replies were also received, and the SIA between routers A and B never would have occurred.

Now that we've pointed out the problem that low-speed NBMA networks can cause, what can we do about it? Does this mean that you cannot have these types of interfaces in your network? Although point-to-point subinterfaces more closely relate the true topology to EIGRP and eliminate these types of problems, multipoint interfaces may be the best network type for some implementations. Instead of banning point-to-multipoint links from the network, two alternatives exist to avoid the timing problem.

First, you can increase the active timer via the command `eigrp timers active-time <time in minutes>` so the retransmission time-out will expire on low-speed multipoint interfaces before the active timer. This is not a recommended solution, because EIGRP will delay converging until the active timer expires in the event of a problem on the network.

The second, and preferred, solution is to decrease the hello interval and hold time on low-speed NBMA networks to 30-second (instead of 60-second) hellos and 90-second (instead of 180-second) hold times. Don't forget to change both! Changing only the hold time without changing the hello interval will almost certainly cause neighbor instability. The commands to change these timers are:

```
interface s0.1 multipoint
  ip eigrp 1 hello-interval 30
  ip eigrp 1 holdtime 90
```

NBMA and Split Horizon

Like all distance vector routing protocols, EIGRP uses split horizon to prevent temporary routing loops while converging. The split-horizon rule states that a router should not advertise destinations out the interface it is using to reach those destinations. For example, in Figure 3.18, the link between routers A, B, and C is a multipoint frame relay network in a hub-and-spoke topology. The hub router, router A, would receive network X from router B but would not advertise it back out to router C, as its next hop is through the same interface.

If you wanted to allow router A to ignore split horizon and to advertise the routes it has learned from router B to router C, you might think that the command `no ip split-horizon` configured on router A's multipoint serial interface would change the behavior. In fact, it doesn't impact EIGRP operation at all! Instead, you must use the EIGRP-specific command `no ip eigrp <AS> split-horizon` instead. Normally, disabling split horizon is not recommended, but occasionally, a legitimate need for disabling the default behavior occurs.

Frame-Relay Broadcast Queue

As frame relay is not broadcast capable, multipoint interfaces duplicate broadcast packets so that each remote attached to the hub router can receive a copy. Quite often, the default broadcast queue will not be large enough to handle the broadcast traffic presented to the interface, and some of the broadcasts will be dropped. As EIGRP packets can be lost because of lack of space on the broadcast queue, the network can become completely destabilized as EIGRP neighbors continually reset.

You can tell whether the broadcast queue is a problem by looking at the output of a `show interface` and evaluating the field highlighted in

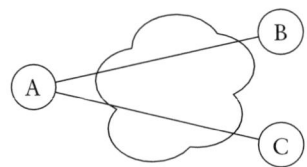

Figure 3.18 Split horizon and multipoint interfaces

Chapter 3: EIGRP Network Design

boldface type in the following sample output. If a significant number of broadcast queue drops are seen on the frame relay interface, tuning the broadcast queue would be an appropriate step.

```
Serial0 is up, line protocol is up
     Hardware is MK5025
     Description: Frame Relay link to Albany DLCI 100
     MTU 1500 bytes, BW 1024 Kbit, DLY 20000 usec, rely
  255/255, load 44/255
     Encapsulation FRAME-RELAY, loopback not set,
  keepalive set (10 sec)
     LMI enq sent 7940, LMI stat recvd 7937, LMI upd
  recvd 0, DTE LMI up
     LMI enq recvd 0, LMI stat sent 0, LMI upd sent 0
     LMI DLCI 1023 LMI type is CISCO frame relay DTE
     Broadcast queue 64/64, broadcasts sent/dropped
  1769202/1849660, interface broadcasts 3579215
```

The command used to change the broadcast queue is:

```
frame-relay broadcast-queue size byte-rate packet-rate
```

The broadcast queue has a maximum transmission rate (throughput) limit measured in both bytes per second and packets per second. The broadcast queue is given priority when broadcasts are being transmitted more slowly than the maximum and therefore has a guaranteed minimum bandwidth allocation. The two transmission rate limits are intended to avoid flooding the interface with broadcasts. The limit is considered reached if the limit for either bytes per second or packets per second is reached. Given the transmission rate restriction, additional buffering is required to store broadcast packets.

The queue size should be set to avoid loss of broadcast (or multicast) routing update packets. The exact size to define depends on the number of packets required for each update. To be safe, the queue size should be set so that one complete routing update for each neighbor can be stored. As a general rule, start with 20 packets per DLCI. The byte rate should be less than both of the following:

- *N*/4 times the minimum remote access rate, measured in bytes per second, where *N* is the number of DLCIs to which the broadcast must be replicated
- One fourth the local access rate, measured in bytes per second

The packet rate is not critical if the byte rate is set conservatively. In general, the packet rate should be set assuming 250-byte packets. The defaults are 64 queue size, 256,000 bytes per second (2,048,000 bits per second), and 36 packets per second.

Dial Backup Strategies

One of the more complicated aspects of designing any network is defining backup strategies. It's seldom acceptable for a remote site to lose connectivity to the core of the network in the event of a link or a router outage. As mentioned earlier, remote sites need to have resilient, redundant connections to the distribution layer, and many networks use dual-homed frame relay PVCs to meet this need.

However, what happens if both frame relay links are down or the router providing access to those links is down? An alternative path must be provided. Therefore, most people create dial strategies to support temporary connections from remote sites lasting only for the duration of the outage of the normal connection path. Two of the many possible strategies that can be used are

- *Dial from remote:* If the remote site routers lose all connectivity through their normal links to the distribution-layer routers they are attached to, they would dial in to a router someplace else on the network.
- *Dial from distribution:* If the distribution-layer router loses all its routing information to a given remote destination, it dials into a router at the remote site.

Beyond deciding which end of the link should initiate the dial backup connection, you must also decide what specific mechanism will be used to start the call. Here again, two options are available.

- *Interesting traffic:* Losing routes causes a floating static route to be installed, which then causes traffic to begin flowing over a

Chapter 3: EIGRP Network Design

dial-on-demand link. Once the router with the dial link begins receiving packets that must traverse the link, that router dials through to the other end so it can forward the traffic.

- *Dialer watch*: A dialer watch is a specific mechanism used by Cisco IOS to dial a backup link when a primary link fails.

All these configurations deal more with configuring dialup links, so we won't cover them here. One point of particular interest in an EIGRP network, though, is how the protocol reacts when both the primary link and the dial backup link are connected. In the network depicted in Figure 3.19, for example, the link between routers A and B has failed, causing the backup link between routers C and D to be brought up. After a period of time, the link between routers A and B is repaired. Let's look at what happens after the link is repaired. Assume that router A is summarizing the routes it learns from routers B and E to 172.20.0.0/16 so router F sees only the summary.

If we aren't also summarizing on router D, F will prefer the path through D to reach components of 172.20.0.0/16, such as 172.20.1.0/24 and 172.20.2.0/24, as long as the dial link between C and D is up. In fact, to make matters worse, if C is advertising 172.20.2.0/24 to D, F will prefer the path through D for 172.20.2.0/24 as well! IP routing uses the most specific route to reach a target; therefore, router F would prefer

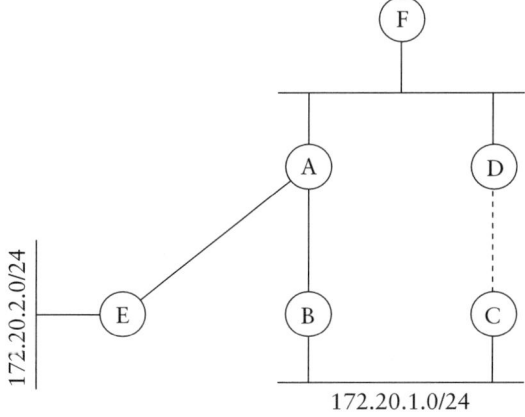

Figure 3.19 Dial backup recovery

the path to 172.20.2.0/24 through router D instead of the 172.20.0.0/16 received from router A, even though A is a smaller metric! When you scale this scenario to hundreds of remotes attached to a single distribution-layer router, it can cause real problems; a single link failing to a single remote can force all the traffic destined to all the remotes attached to the same distribution-layer router through the dial backup link.

The obvious solution is to summarize on router D, right? Not exactly. Now router E will have two paths to the 172.20.0.0/16 network and will either always choose the path through router A, even though 172.20.1.0/24 is no longer reachable that way, or will load share between the paths through routers A and D.

Not summarizing doesn't work, and summarizing doesn't work. What's left? You can build a distribution list on router C, allowing it to advertise only the 172.20.1.0/24 network to router D. With no summarization, only traffic destined to this one network will pass through the dialup link, leaving us with one other problem, though: How do we get the link to stop passing traffic altogether?

As long as the dial link is operational, router E will see the path through router D as the best way to reach the 172.20.1.0/24 network. It doesn't matter what the metrics are in this case, because the route advertised by router D is more specific (24-bit prefix length) than the route advertised by router A (16-bit prefix length). Generally speaking, this issue can't be resolved using an EIGRP solution. Instead, you will need to configure the dial link to be brought down if traffic is flowing in only one direction (interesting traffic) or if the serial interface on router B is up.

Redistribution Issues

In its simplest form, an EIGRP network would contain nothing but native, internal EIGRP routes. In the real world, however, an all-EIGRP network is rare. For various reasons, most networks contain multiple routing protocols, from a few simple static routes to multiple routing protocols with mutual redistribution at multiple points in the network. Redistribution will always bring complexity to an EIGRP network, but if done correctly, it can be handled with few problems.

EIGRP has many types of redistribution, and the following sections discuss the operation and complexity of a couple of them, including redistribution with IGRP (same autonomous system) and EIGRP (different autonomous system). Each section describes the normal operation and expected behavior, along with problems to watch out for and actions to take to decrease the possible problems. But first, we'll have a brief discussion on redistribution in general.

General Issues

Redistribution is required when routes learned through one routing protocol must be propagated through another routing protocol. Following are some of the reasons redistribution between protocols might be required:

- Transitioning from one routing protocol to another
- A mix of devices supporting various routing protocols on the network
- The merger of companies using different routing protocols
- Bad network design

Route redistribution in a network is of four general forms:

- One-way redistribution
- Mutual redistribution at one point in the network
- Mutual redistribution at multiple points between two networks
- Mutual redistribution between multiple networks at multiple places

Before reviewing each of these forms of route redistribution and describing the unique challenges each brings to the network design, we need to discuss a complication brought about by performing redistribution between EIGRP and routing protocols that are not capable of supporting routes with variable-length subnet masks.

As discussed in Chapter 1, EIGRP is capable of distributing routes with **VLSM (variable-length subnet masks)** because it includes the subnet mask for each route in the updates that it sends to its neighbors.

Problems can arise, however, when VLSM-based EIGRP routes are redistributed into a routing protocol that is not capable of supporting VLSM networks, such as RIPv1 or IGRP. In the following discussion, we will use IGRP in our examples, but the same complications also hold true for RIPv1.

In Figure 3.20, both the EIGRP and the IGRP portions of the network contain subnets of network 10.0.0.0/8, and EIGRP uses a number of masks for its subnets of that network (/24 and /26 masks). IGRP, on the other hand, cannot handle different masks and thus uses only /24 masks. When router A tries to redistribute the /26 routes into IGRP, IGRP will be unable to propagate them to its neighbors. Why is EIGRP able to handle the different masks and IGRP unable to?

The problem lies in the fact that IGRP (and RIPv1) do not include the mask associated with each route in update packets. Therefore, IGRP has no way to communicate which mask should be associated with each of the routes it is sending to its neighbors. Because of the lack of explicit information, IGRP (and RIPv1) assume that each route in an update packet belongs to either

- The same major network as one or more interfaces on this router—assumes that it has the same subnet mask as the router for that major network

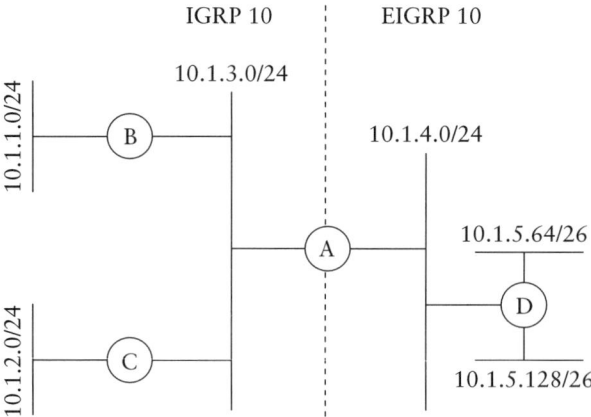

Figure 3.20 Redistribution between IGRP and EIGRP

Chapter 3: EIGRP Network Design

- A major network that isn't on any interface of this router—the route uses the classful mask associated with the major network

Therefore, any of the redistributed routes in our sample network in Figure 3.20 with the /26 mask will be discarded by the IGRP process in router A.

One possible solution to this problem is to create a static route on router A to "summarize" the /26 routes from EIGRP into a route that matches the /24 mask used in the IGRP part of the network. For example, router A could contain the static route `ip route 10.1.5.0 255.255.255.0 null0` and redistribute it into IGRP. Router A would give the IGRP routers the /24 route they can use and propagate. When a packet is destined to a host on the 10.1.5.64 subnet, IGRP would use the /24 route to get the packet to router A. Router A, in turn, would have the EIGRP routes for 10.1.5.64/26 and 10.1.5.128/26, so it could complete the delivery of the packets to the correct destinations.

Another possible solution is to use a default-network strategy in IGRP, so any target route not contained in the IGRP routing updates will be sent to the default network, which would be the routers doing redistribution from EIGRP to IGRP. All routers in the IGRP part of the network must be using "ip classless" in order for this strategy to work. Unfortunately, if a "true" default network exists in the IGRP part of the network, such as a link to the Internet, this alternative will not work. IGRP would be unable to identify which targets should be sent to the IGRP/EIGRP redistribution point and which should be sent to the Internet access point.

If the non-VLSM part of the network is RIPv1 instead of IGRP, a solution would be to convert it to RIPv2, which supports variable-length subnet masks. Another alternative would be to send a default route (0.0.0.0/0) from the redistributing router into the RIP portion of the network. Similar to the default-network option described for IGRP, this alternative would allow the RIPv1 routers to send all packets destined for target subnets not contained in the routing table to the redistributing router. The same requirement for "ip classless" and the same limitation if there is a "true" default location hold true for the default route strategy in RIPv1.

One more point on this subject. The preceding limitation exists only if the same major network exists in both the EIGRP part and the non-VLSM part of the network. If you are using VLSM in the EIGRP part of the network and are redistributing only the major network into a non-VLSM-capable protocol, this problem doesn't exist. Only the major network should be sent across the redistribution point, so the non-VLSM protocol should be able to handle it just fine.

Now that we've discussed a general problem with redistribution owing to the different capabilities in different routing protocols, we will discuss specific forms of redistribution and the complications each one brings.

Forms of Redistribution

One-Way Redistribution: Often, a network will contain devices that must receive routes in a routing protocol other than EIGRP but that don't need to supply any routes back into EIGRP. A typical example of this scenario is UNIX workstations running `routed` in quiet mode in order to receive and make local decisions based on routes learned through RIP. In this case, the core of the network may be EIGRP, and the EIGRP routes may be redistributed into RIP at the edges in order to provide routes to the UNIX workstations.

Another example of one-way redistribution is static routes redistributed into an EIGRP network. You may not consider static routes a routing protocol, but when planning for redistribution and filtering, you must consider them as a source of external routes into EIGRP.

ODR can also be redistributed into EIGRP to propagate routes originated at remote sites. Default routing would be used on the remotes to deliver packets into the hub of the network, so EIGRP routes do not need to be redistributed into ODR. In reality, routes cannot be redistributed into ODR at all, so like redistributed static routes, ODR by definition means that there is one-way redistribution.

In one-way redistribution, there is seldom any concern for routing loops or network instability created by a mistaken view of the network. This is by far the safest form of redistribution in a network.

Mutual Redistribution at a Single Point: The second form of route redistribution is mutual redistribution at one point in the network. Figure 3.21 shows an RIP network connected to an EIGRP network, with one router

Chapter 3: EIGRP Network Design

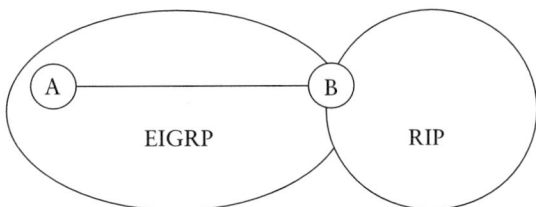

Figure 3.21 Mutual redistribution at a single point

doing the redistribution. RIP routes are redistributed into EIGRP, and EIGRP routes are redistributed into RIP. With the exception of the problems introduced by connecting a classful routing protocol to a classless routing protocol, mutual redistribution at one point in the network is relatively safe.

You should put filters in place so that routes originating in the RIP domain cannot be relearned inbound in the EIGRP domain, and vice-versa, but the filters are probably unnecessary. The route-redistribution process will normally successfully make the right decisions about where routes should point, and instability should not be a major problem.

Mutual Redistribution at Multiple Points between Two Networks: This is where it becomes more of a challenge to make sure that routing instability isn't caused by the loss of information arising from redistribution. For example, because RIP's metric (hop count) has no direct relationship to EIGRP's metric, a somewhat arbitrary metric needs to be artificially applied when routes are redistributed between these protocols. Therefore, the true topological distance required to reach a target network will be lost in the redistribution process, causing the possibility of suboptimal routing or routing loops.

Additionally, when a route is redistributed from one protocol into another at multiple points, the same route may be received on a router from multiple sources from multiple protocols. The router must sort out what the right thing to do is. Combined with the loss of metric information and the various convergence characteristics of various routing protocols, a routing loop or other problems are almost certain.

The most obvious way to prevent problems with mutual redistribution at multiple points is to use `distribute-lists` between the routing protocols to prevent feeding routes through multiple redistributions. You can also tag the routes, using an EIGRP administrative tag to stop half of this type of routing loop by preventing EIGRP from redistributing external routes back into their original protocol.

Mutual Redistribution between Multiple Networks at Multiple Points: Figure 3.22 shows multiple parts of the network running one routing protocol (IGRP in this case), all connecting at multiple places to a single area of the network running EIGRP. This scenario is a variation of mutual redistribution at multiple points, with the added complexity that many routes will be coming into EIGRP as external routes, will get redistributed into another routing protocol, and will then be relearned from another entry point into EIGRP as a different external route. This can bring disaster! Filtering is absolutely necessary in this scenario in order to increase the odds of stability.

Administrative Distance

One of the ways in which Cisco IOS increases stability and decreases the likelihood of routing loops is through the use of *administrative distances (ADs)* assigned to each protocol. The term *distance* is a bit of a misnomer, as it seems to imply how far something is; in fact, the AD has nothing to do with the metric or path selection within a protocol. Instead, AD refers to *the believability of a route learned via a particular protocol*. The lower the AD, the more believable the route.

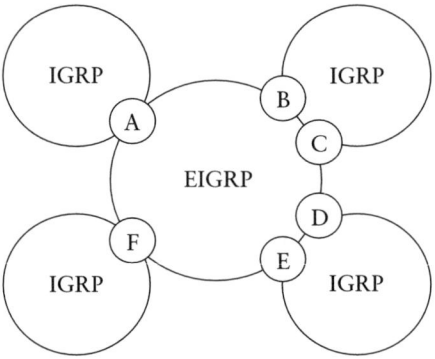

Figure 3.22 Mutual redistribution between multiple networks at multiple points

Chapter 3: EIGRP Network Design

Table 3.2 shows the relative ADs for IP routing protocols. As you would expect, directly connected routes are the most believable—they exist on this router!—with static routes being the next most believable. Cisco IOS assumes that routes configured by hand should be considered believable!

The AD is used when installing routes in the routing table to decide which one of several matching routes will be installed. For instance, if RIP and EIGRP both attempt to install a route to 10.1.1.0/24, assuming that the EIGRP route is internal, the EIGRP route will be installed. If, however, RIP attempted to install a route to 10.1.1.0/24 and EIGRP attempted to install a route to 10.1.0.0/16, *both* routes would be installed successfully, because they are not the same route.

The AD is a deciding factor only when both the prefix and the prefix length match. When redistributing between protocols, it's important to understand how the AD will influence the routes chosen by the router when it's presented with two paths to the same destination.

Table 3.2. Administrative Distances

Route Source	AD
Connected	0
Static	1
EIGRP Summary	5
External BGP	20
Internal EIGRP	90
IGRP	100
OSPF	110
IS-IS	115
RIP	120
EGP	140
ODR	160
External EIGRP	170
Internal BGP	200
Unknown	255

Two commands can be issued in Cisco IOS to modify the administrative distance of routes received from certain neighbors or via certain protocols. For most protocols other than EIGRP, the distance of routes received via a particular protocol can be changed with the following command:

```
router rip
 distance <distance> [address|access-list]
```

Because EIGRP uses two administrative distances for routes, the syntax of the command is slightly different. Internal and external routes may have their administrative distances set individually. With EIGRP, unfortunately, you cannot limit which routes get this change based on neighbor or access list, as you can in the preceding example. The EIGRP form of the command is

```
router eigrp 1
 distance eigrp <internal> <external>
```

A word of caution is in order at this point: *Be very careful when you decide to change the default administrative distances.* Make *very* sure that you understand the ramifications of the changes, and verify through thorough testing that the behavior will be what you expect.

Source of Redistributed Routes

One additional comment on redistribution needs to be stated. As described in Chapter 2, all redistribution is performed from the routing table. This very important concept is often the source of confusion when routes are not filtered or redistributed in the manner you might expect. For example, if you receive a route to 10.1.1.0/24 via both RIP and OSPF and then redistribute RIP into EIGRP, 10.1.1.0/24 will not be propagated into EIGRP. The path through OSPF will win the AD test (110 for OSPF and 120 for RIP), so the path through RIP will not be installed in the routing table. As it goes to redistribute RIP-derived routes into its topology table, EIGRP looks in the routing table, doesn't find 10.1.1.0/24 as a RIP route, and thus doesn't redistribute it.

Similarly, you cannot tell a routing protocol to limit the routes it is redistributing into another protocol. In other words, you cannot tell EIGRP to not redistribute certain routes into OSPF. Again, all redistribution is done from the routing table and is done by the outbound routing protocol. If you want to influence which routes from EIGRP are redistributed into OSPF, you must tell OSPF about it. Redistribution filters can be applied only as a routing protocol is pulling routes out of the routing table.

This behavior is important to understand when deciding how to redistribute and filter redistributed routes. More on this aspect of redistribution will be covered later. Now that we've discussed some general redistribution issues, let's move on to specific cases and how each one behaves.

IGRP in the Same Autonomous System: In almost every case of redistribution, you must manually configure EIGRP to redistribute routes learned from other routing protocols. The only exception when you redistribute between EIGRP and IGRP is if they belong to the same autonomous system. In this case, redistribution is automatic and can be disabled only via the commands

```
router eigrp <autonomous system>
  no redistribute igrp <autonomous system>
```

When routes are taken from IGRP, the metric is scaled by 256, as EIGRP uses a 32-bit number to represent the metric and IGRP uses a 16-bit number. When it is moved into EIGRP, the IGRP route is identified as an external route with an administrative distance of 170. In the external data section of the EIGRP topology table entry, the advertising router—the router that redistributed the IGRP route into EIGRP—is identified as well as the original IGRP metric of the route.

One additional unique property of IGRP/EIGRP redistribution within the same autonomous system is the interesting case when the administrative distance of the routes is ignored. Here is the one exception to the AD rule! If a route is learned through EIGRP as an external (AD of 170) and IGRP (AD of 100), within the same autonomous system number, the AD is ignored, and the metric, after scaling between IGRP and EIGRP, alone is used to determine the preferred path.

This exception to administrative distance was implemented in order to avoid routing loops while transitioning from IGRP to EIGRP. For example, in Figure 3.23, several clouds of IGRP networks are connected

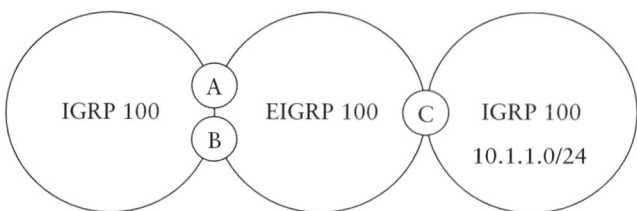

Figure 3.23 Administrative distance in IGRP-to-EIGRP redistribution

to a core of EIGRP. This situation may be short-lived during a transition from IGRP to EIGRP, or it could remain for a period of time. Let's look at what would happen if the exception to the administrative distance rules didn't exist.

As the route to 10.1.1.0/24 is redistributed into EIGRP by router C from the IGRP cloud on the right, the route goes from having an administrative distance of 100 for IGRP to 170 for an EIGRP external. As it passes through the EIGRP cloud and is redistributed into the IGRP cloud on the left by router A, the route becomes an IGRP route again, which doesn't have any concept of an external route, and thus has an administrative distance of 100.

Router B will now have two routes to 10.1.1.0/24—one through IGRP as it was redistributed by router A and an EIGRP external as it was redistributed by router C. Which route should router B choose? According to normal processing using the administrative distances of the two routes, the IGRP route would be preferred! This is obviously incorrect.

Instead, the behavior was changed so that router C, when it receives the same route as an EIGRP external and through IGRP, compares the metric—with the IGRP metric scaled by 256—in order to determine which path is the most direct to the target network. In this case, the EIGRP external route to 10.1.1.0/24 would be preferred and would be installed in router C's routing table, even though it has a higher administrative distance than the IGRP route.

With this somewhat nonintuitive behavior, redistribution between IGRP and EIGRP in the same autonomous system is fairly safe and normally will provide the desired functionality. This built-in safeguard will keep poor next-hop selections from being made and will normally create a stable network. The following section describes a much different picture.

Multiple EIGRP Autonomous Systems: It's fairly common to see large EIGRP networks divided into a number of separate EIGRP autonomous systems with mutual redistribution between them. This may be done for three reasons:

- Defining the scope of administrative control, with each autonomous system controlled by a different group of people
- Merging companies
- Attempting to reduce query range

In the first and second cases, the reason chosen for multiple autonomous systems is more of a political or a management decision, not a technical decision. In reality, if multiple EIGRP autonomous systems are used with mutual redistribution between them, very little in the way of protection or autonomy is provided. Unless other techniques, such as summarization or distribution lists, are used, a link flap in one AS will be felt in the other autonomous systems as well. If summarization or route filtering is used to stop this propagation from happening, the information hiding through summarization/filtering—not the multiple autonomous systems—is making the network more robust.

The third reason is probably the most common one for choosing to implement multiple EIGRP autonomous systems. During the early days of EIGRP, network instability owing to SIA routes was extremely common, and not many tools were available to stop the problems. By defining multiple EIGRP autonomous systems, the timing of the SIA process is indeed changed a little, and a minor increase in network stability could be the result. Unfortunately, the complexity of route redistribution and the routing loops caused by the redistribution are far more harmful than the benefits gained.

First, the benefits of multiple autonomous systems will be explained. Figure 3.24 shows a network comprising multiple EIGRP autonomous systems with mutual redistribution between them. When the route to 172.20.40.0/24 on the left goes active owing to a link flap, queries flow throughout AS 1, looking for an alternative path to reach this network.

88 EIGRP for IP: Basic Operation and Configuration

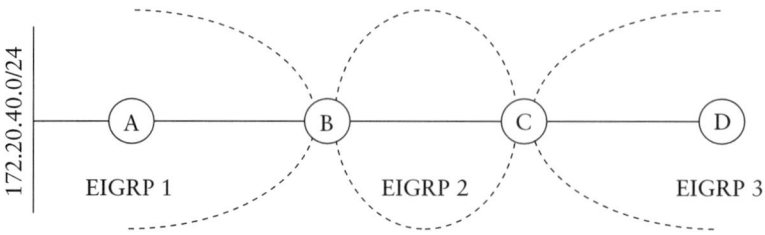

Figure 3.24 Mutual redistribution between multiple EIGRP ASs

When the query reaches router B, it replies to the original query but then starts another one of its own in AS 2. When this query reaches the router C, the second query process is terminated via a reply, but a new query process is started in AS 3!

The timing of the query process has been changed. Instead of router A waiting for a reply until router D has finished processing the query, router A receives a reply when router B processes the query. A second and then a third query process are started independently, and each must be terminated in order to successfully converge on the topology change. At least the router that originally asked the question will not get an SIA due to a link problem in the third AS!

The good news is that the router that originated the query won't generate an SIA. The bad news is that redistribution between multiple EIGRP autonomous systems creates very significant complexities and can cause much harm. Let's take a fairly simple example. In Figure 3.25, we again have multiple EIGRP autonomous systems connected via multiple points of entry, as well as a cloud of RIP routers in our network. When the route to network 172.20.40.0/24 is originated in RIP, the route has an AD of 120 throughout the RIP domain. When it is redistributed into EIGRP AS 1 by router B, the route becomes an external route and thus has an AD of 170 throughout AS 1. The route is then advertised into AS 2 by router C, where it continues to have an AD of 170. Here's where it gets interesting.

Thanks to the redistribution in router C, the route to 172.20.40.0/24 will be learned on router D from two directions: as an external route via AS 1 and as an external route via AS 2. So which path will win on router D: the one through AS 1 or the one through AS 2? Logic says that the

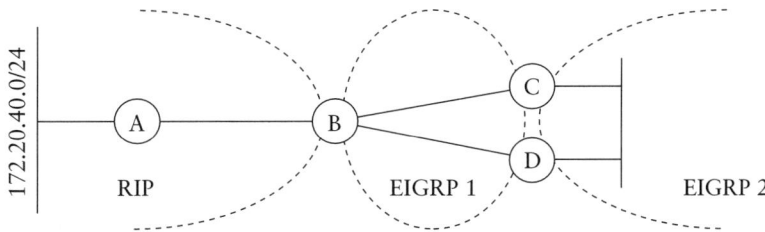

Figure 3.25 Multiple EIGRP autonomous systems

path through AS 1 will win because it is obviously a shorter path: It has a smaller metric through AS 1 than through AS 2.

Unfortunately, this isn't how it works. Routing protocols use the metric to select a path between alternative paths within a single instance of a routing protocol. If the same route—prefix and prefix length—is learned via two routing protocols, the metric is ignored! The exception, as described earlier, is for routes learned via EIGRP (external) and IGRP in the same autonomous system. Other than this exception, the metric plays no part in path selection when comparing routes learned via different routing protocols, including multiple EIGRP autonomous systems! So how is the path selection made?

The path selection criterion, as described earlier, is the administrative distance. The path learned via the routing protocol with the lowest AD will be the one put into the routing table. But wait! In our example, the path to 172.20.40.0/24 is learned on router D from both EIGRP AS 1 and EIGRP AS 2 as externals, so both routes have an AD of 170. Which one wins? Unfortunately, the result will not be consistent: Whichever route is installed in the routing table first will win.

How can you avoid this problem? Careful route filtering at the redistribution points is required to keep these feedback loops from creating havoc in your network. The next section discusses the most common method of performing route filtering at these redistribution points: *distribution lists*.

Route Filtering: Earlier, route filtering was described as a method of hiding information in order to decrease query scope and complexity in the network. Route filtering can also be used to eliminate the propagation, or acceptance, of routes that would create routing loops or suboptimal routing in a network. For example, route filters are commonly used at redistribution points in order to make certain there won't be routing loops owing to AD problems. This use is crucial when there are multiple points of redistribution between multiple routing protocols.

An example of the damage that can be caused is depicted in Figure 3.26, which shows the route to 172.20.40.0/24 entering EIGRP as an external and flowing through AS 1, having an AD of 170 on each EIGRP router. As the route is redistributed from EIGRP AS 1 into AS 2, it continues to have an AD value of 170. The problems begin when the route is redistributed by router C into AS 2; router D receives two EIGRP external routes, both with an AD of 170, and must choose between the two. Which one gets installed? The answer is indeterminate: There is no way of knowing which one will be installed. The one that is installed, however, will be redistributed into the other AS; for example, if router D decides to install the AS 2 route in its routing table, router D will redistribute the AS 2 route back into AS 1.

The only way to make certain the right route is installed is to put a distribution list inbound under AS 2 on the routers redistributing between AS 2 and AS 1, denying the routes that originated in AS 1, originally a RIP route, from being learned inbound from AS 2. This configuration can be administratively troublesome, keeping these access lists correct as network changes occur, but it needs to happen in order to ensure that routing is correct.

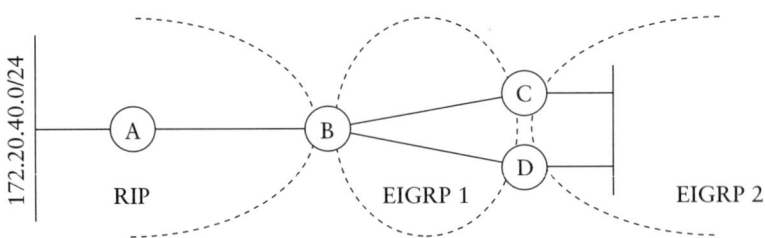

Figure 3.26 Route filters to prevent routing loops

Other Design Considerations

We've now covered a number of design issues that must be considered when designing an EIGRP network, but a couple of other design questions are often asked by people building networks using EIGRP. These common questions will be discussed in this section.

Probably the most frequently asked question is, How many neighbors are too many for an EIGRP router? Considerable cost savings are possible in having as many remote sites connect to the same distribution router as possible, particularly if the traffic requirements for each remote site are fairly small and regular. Early in the life of EIGRP, Cisco typically recommended no more than 30 neighbors per router, but this limit obviously doesn't support the density required by networks today.

With proper design, an EIGRP router will reliably support many more than 30 neighbors. How many more can be supported? It depends! It depends on how much information is being sent to the remotes, whether the remotes are stub sites, the speed of the links, the stability of the network, and a myriad other factors. Unfortunately, we cannot state a magic number to use or even a magic formula to apply to determine the maximum allowable neighbors. Instead, we will discuss how each factor influences the maximum number of neighbors so that you can make a reasonable estimate of how many neighbors a router can handle.

The first consideration is how many routes must be exchanged with each remote router. If the remote site has a single link to the remainder of the network, it really doesn't need any! A default route on the remote router will suffice to send traffic to the distribution router and will need to advertise to the distribution router only whatever routes originate at the remote site.

In Figure 3.27, router A can reach the rest of the network only through the connection between the two routers, so a default route pointing to router B is all that's necessary for passing traffic into the network from the remote site. Router A would be responsible for sending in the routes located at the remote site so distribution router B can propagate them to the remainder of the network. In this case, very little routing update traffic would be required with any remote site.

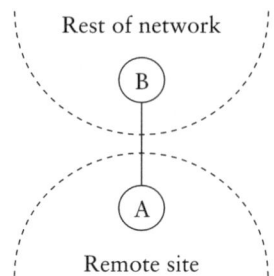

Figure 3.27 A simple remote site routing situation

If the remote site requires receiving at least a single route for its dial backup strategy to work properly, the preceding holds true. The distribution router B would send a single default route to router A, and router A would send its local routes to router B. Again, very little routing information would need to be passed to the remotes.

In both of these scenarios, the amount of update traffic to the remotes is very small. Unfortunately, unless the remote routers are defined as stub routers, all these remote routers would still be involved in the query process. Distribution lists and summary statements limiting updates from router B to router A will limit updates to a single default—or even nothing—but that will not stop queries. By defining the remote routers as stub routers, even queries will not be sent to the remote sites.

A third scenario is if the remote site has dual frame relay PVCs and needs at least some routes from each distribution site, as shown in Figure 3.28. This situation may happen if the two frame relay circuits terminate at distribution routers that are geographically dispersed and there is significant delay or congestion to send traffic to the "wrong" distribution router. In this case, more routes must be exchanged with each remote site, increasing the work EIGRP must perform. In this type of network, distribution lists *must* be put on the remote routes so remotes do not reflect routes learned from one distribution router back to the other distribution router.

The fourth scenario is if the network is not hierarchical and remote sites are connected to one another. These "back-door" links can be fully meshed or partially meshed. In this scenario, far more routing knowledge

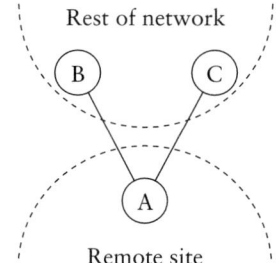

Figure 3.28 Dual-homed remotes

is required on the routers in order to select the correct next hop, and the complexity of the query path is dramatically increased. EIGRP's job can be extremely difficult in this type of network.

Besides the route count and complexity, other factors influencing how many neighbors are allowable include the CPU power of the routers involved, the stability of the network, and the link speeds to reach those remote sites. If links are not stable or are congested or if routers are underpowered, EIGRP will be less likely to respond quickly to topology changes and will more likely be unable to converge successfully.

As the complexity and route requirements increase, you should decrease the number of neighbors. With only default routing and high-powered distribution routers, such as RSP4s or 7200s with NPE300s, we've successfully tested in the lab with 500 neighbors! Other networks cannot retain stability with 10–20 neighbors if there are many routes, no hierarchy, route reflection, and unstable links. Using the simplifying techniques described in this chapter, 300 neighbors have been implemented successfully in a production network.

4

EIGRP Troubleshooting

We've looked at how EIGRP works, configuring and running EIGRP, and EIGRP network design. With all of this theory in the background, let's look at some common problems you might see in an EIGRP network and consider how to troubleshoot them. In this chapter, we'll look at

- Problems with neighbor relationships
- Stuck in Active routes
- Duplicate router IDs
- Failure to converge

We'll start by looking at various problems you might encounter with building and maintaining neighbor relationships.

Problems with Neighbor Relationships

You may recall from Chapter 1 that EIGRP uses neighbor relationships to control the exchange of routing information and to ensure the validity of routes received from a given neighbor. These neighbor relationships are built using a simple hello protocol. A neighbor relationship between two routers running EIGRP can break down in several ways:

- One-way communication: The link between two routers running EIGRP has failed in such a way that traffic is passed in only one direction.

- Unicast only: The link between the EIGRP neighbors has failed so that only unicast traffic is passed.

- **Multicast only:** The link between the EIGRP neighbors has failed, so only multicast traffic succeeds in passing between them. Or, only multicast traffic is passed in one direction, whereas all other traffic is passed in the other direction.

- **Overburdened or dirty link:** The link between the two routers is overburdened or is experiencing a high error rate, so a lot of EIGRP packets are dropped or lost.

One-Way Communication between Two Routers

One-way failures on a link are unusual, but they do happen, because most network types consist of two unidirectional links tied together as one link. If you lose the right pair on Ethernet or have the right type of failure on a frame relay link and conditions are otherwise right, traffic will pass in one direction but not in the other across the link.

If this type of a problem occurs before the two routers attached to the link begin communicating, the neighbor relationship will never form. If this type of problem occurs in the middle of a running network, when the routers on either side of the link have already formed a neighbor relationship, the problems can be a bit more difficult to recognize.

The following are typical symptoms for one-way communications between routers running EIGRP:

- One router will show the other router as a neighbor but will have a number in the query count, a very high RTO (probably 5,000), and a very low SRTT (probably 0).

- The router on the other end of the link won't see any neighbors across this link.

For example, the network shown in Figure 4.1 contains just two routers. If the link between these routers failed such that A could transmit to B but B couldn't transmit to A, we would see the following output when executing a `show ip eigrp neighbor` on A:

```
routera#show ip eigrp neighbors
    IP-EIGRP neighbors for process 2
    H Address     Interface   Hold Uptime   SRTT   RTO   Q    Seq
                              (sec)         (ms)         Cnt  Num
```

Chapter 4: EIGRP Troubleshooting

Figure 4.1 One-way communication example

It's not very exciting: A doesn't show any neighbors at all. On B, issuing `show ip eigrp neighbors` gives us something more interesting to look at:

```
routerb#show ip eigrp neighbors

IP-EIGRP neighbors for process 2
H   Address     Interface   Hold  Uptime    SRTT  RTO   Q    Seq
                            (sec)           (ms)        Cnt  Num
0   10.1.1.1    Et1         11    00:01:02  0     5000  112  0
```

B shows A as a neighbor, but the SRTT is 0, the RTO is 5,000, and the query count is 112. All these are signs that these two routers aren't successfully passing traffic between them. The only solution to this type of problem is to troubleshoot the link between the routers and to repair it. Neighbor relationships will never work correctly over a link that passes traffic in only one direction.

Unicast-Only between Two Routers

Some types of links may fail in such a way that allows unicast traffic to be delivered but not multicast and broadcast packets. ATM, SMDS, frame relay, and other nonbroadcast types of networks are where you're likely to see this sort of failure.

Again, if two routers that haven't ever been neighbors are attached to a link with no multicast capabilities, the symptoms will be rather obvious: Neither router will show any neighbors across the failed link. If two routers have built a neighbor relationship over a link before the failure occurs, they will probably drop their neighbor relationship eventually, owing to hold time expiration, but it may take a while for the relationship to fail. Why? Let's look at Figure 4.2.

Let's assume that a large number of dialup users are behind router C, causing the EIGRP routing table to change every 10 seconds or so. These changes would be passed on the router B, then to router A, where

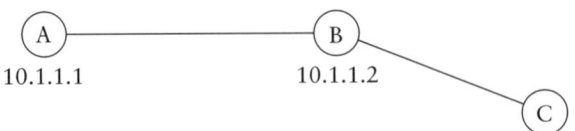

Figure 4.2 A unicast-only link failure

they are filtered through summarization. With each change, B would send a multicast query or update to A and then wait for an acknowledgment. B will never receive that acknowledgment—multicast packets aren't getting delivered across this link—so its retransmit timer will time out, resulting in a unicast retransmission. When it receives this packet, A resets the hold timer on B, as receiving any EIGRP packet is just as good as receiving a hello packet.

A, in turn, will send an acknowledgment for this packet back to B, which will reset B's hold timer for A. Again, the same rule applies: The acknowledgment, sent unicast, is as good as a hello packet in maintaining the neighbor relationship.

The neighbors would probably time out eventually, owing to hold timer expiration, as it's almost impossible to envision a network with this much activity, but it could take some time. Once the neighbors have timed out, the neighbor relationship wouldn't be rebuilt until multicast forwarding had been repaired.

The easiest way to check for this condition is to ping the EIGRP multicast address—224.0.0.10. You should receive an answer from every connected router running EIGRP. The most common cause for this type of problem is a misconfiguration. For instance, ATM and Frame relay both require the *broadcast* keyword in the map statements to deliver broadcast and multicast packets across a point-to-multipoint link.

LANE (LAN emulation) on ATM requires an operational **BUS (broadcast and unknown server)** to successfully send multicast packets. SMDS requires a broadcast mapping to a special PVC to send broadcast and multicast.

In any case, the first thing to do when this type of problem arises is to check all the configurations on all the routers connected to the circuit. Then check the circuit itself, as this is most likely where the problem lies.

Chapter 4: EIGRP Troubleshooting

Multicast-Only between Two Routers

Although you might expect this situation to be impossible—a link that can pass multicast or broadcast traffic but not unicast traffic—it isn't. Some types of networks can fail in such a way so this scenario occurs, and misconfigured or broken routing can produce the same results. Let's use the network in Figure 4.3, which looks remarkably similar to the network in Figure 4.2, as an example.

One routing error that can cause this condition is router B's having a route inserted in its table for 10.1.1.1 pointing toward router C. This can occur if a static host route is configured on router B, such as

```
ip route 10.1.1.1 255.255.255.255 10.1.2.1
```

Any unicast traffic generated by router B toward 10.1.1.1 will be sent to router C instead of to router A, causing symptoms that appear to be identical to unicast not operating correctly between these routers, whereas multicast works correctly.

Another configuration error that can exhibit itself as multicast traffic being delivered correctly and unicast traffic failing is duplicate IP addresses on a multiaccess network. For example, if a station joins the network between router A and router B in Figure 4.3 and is misconfigured to have the IP address 10.1.1.1, it will cause at least intermittent unicast failures when router B tries to deliver replies, acknowledgments, or unicast updates to router A.

You can identify this condition in a way that is similar to the method to recognize one-way traffic. With this problem, however, both routers will see each other in their neighbor tables, but both will show a high query count, 0 SRTT, and 5,000 RTO. The receipt of hello packets will cause the routers to list each other as neighbors, but the failure to deliver any unicast packets will prevent either router from calculating the SRTT or the RTO and from delivering any routing information to the other router.

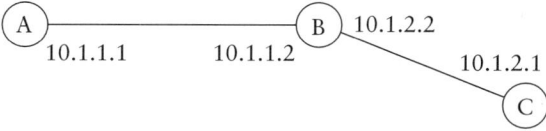

Figure 4.3 Multicast-only traffic owing to a routing error

The best way to resolve this type of problem is to resolve the misconfiguration or to repair the link. It is useful to check the routing table for the neighbor's IP address specifically, because examining the routing table's entry for the attached network won't show you any bad host routes.

Overburdened or Dirty Link

An overburdened link can also cause problems in building an EIGRP neighbor relationship, primarily because the routers can't get hello and other packets through to their neighbors. If the routers can't get any packets through the link, the neighbors will eventually reset owing to a hello timer expiration, which shows up on the router's console if you have configured `eigrp log-neighbor-changes`.

A link that drops most of the EIGRP packets transmitted but does deliver enough to maintain the neighbor relationship would show

- *Regularly missing EIGRP hello packets:* By monitoring the output of `show ip eigrp neighbor`, you can look at the `Hold` column to determine whether a router is failing to receive EIGRP hello packets. If this column consistently drops below the hold time minus the hello time, the router isn't receiving all the hello packets being sent.

- *Continually having data outstanding:* By monitoring the output of `show ip eigrp neighbor`, you can determine whether a router is having problems transmitting data to a neighbor. If the `Q Cnt` column of the output always has a number in it, the router is likely often waiting for acknowledgments for data it has sent.

A poor link between two routers can also show up by causing EIGRP Stuck in Active events elsewhere in the network: The best remedy for this type of problem is to simply fix the link between the two routers. If it's overburdened, find a way to direct traffic through another link or upgrade the link's bandwidth.

You can work around an overburdened link to some degree by turning on Selective Packet Discard, which gives priority to incoming control traffic over incoming data traffic, but this mechanism isn't designed

Chapter 4: EIGRP Troubleshooting

to provide a long-term fix to overburdened links. You can examine the interface counters on the router to determine what the link's problem is and how to resolve it.

Stuck in Active Routes

As discussed, EIGRP uses a query process to find paths to destinations for which it has lost its only known loop-free path(s). Destinations for which a router is actively searching paths to are placed in an *active* state. Because a network cannot converge on the best path toward a given destination while in this active state, the total length of time a route may stay in this state needs to be limited.

The total length of time a route may remain in the active state is called the *Stuck in Active* time, and a route that has been active for this period of time is called an SIA route. SIAs produce console messages, such as

```
%DUAL-3-SIA: Route 10.1.1.0 stuck-in-active state in
   IP-EIGRP 100. Cleaning up
```

SIAs also cause the router to clear the EIGRP neighbor relationship with the router that didn't answer the query within the SIA timer. As you can imagine, this can be a rather destructive process. The SIA timer is, by default, 3 minutes. Two questions need to be answered whenever a route is marked SIA.

- Why did the route go active?
- Why did the route stay active for 3 minutes?

Why Did the Route Go Active?

What network event caused EIGRP to mark the route active? Finding this event may help stabilize the network and prevent further problems. Following are some common reasons routes go active:

- Flapping link
- Dial circuits connecting/disconnecting
- Lost neighbor relationship between two routers

The route that was declared SIA should be closely investigated to see what caused it to be marked active. If there are multiple SIAs, a flapping link, or neighbor relationship, is a likely event to look for. (Refer back to the design concepts suggested in Chapter 3 to find ways of reducing the number of routers affected by a link flap or other activity that causes a route to go active.) Summarization and information hiding are the most effective ways to reduce the number of SIAs in your network.

Why Did the Route Stay Active So Long?

People generally concentrate their efforts on this part of an SIA, as it's the most obvious part of the equation. Troubleshooting an SIA by chasing it through the network can be easy or very difficult. For hub-and-spoke, or strongly hierarchical, networks, chasing an SIA generally involves the following steps.

1. Start with the router that is recording the SIA events.
2. Watch for routes that are active and staying active for 2 minutes or more. You can use the output of `show ip eigrp topology active` to gather this information.
3. TELNET to the neighbor from which this router is waiting on replies. There could be several of these, so you may need to chase the problems in several directions, one at a time. You should obviously start with the router that is most often the one slow in answering. If the route to the node in question is down, use a hop-by-hop approach, connecting sequentially to each router in the path through which the connection to the desired node is achieved. Another way to gain access to a node to which no route exists is to use an out-of-band connection. The hop-by-hop method (or out-of-band access) should be used if a direct TELNET connection is not manageable.
4. Repeat this process for each router in the chain until you find the router or pair of routers that seem to be at the root of the problem.

For a more practical example, we'll work through this process with the network illustrated in Figure 4.4. Let's begin with router A receiving `DUAL-3-SIA` messages on its console for network 10.1.6.0/24. If we TELNET in and run `show ip eigrp topo act`, we see:

Chapter 4: EIGRP Troubleshooting

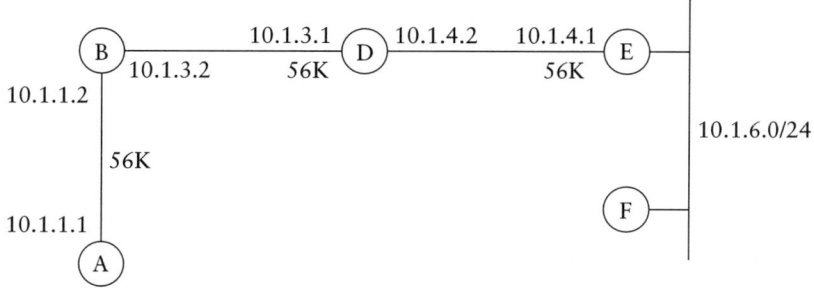

Figure 4.4 Chasing a Stuck in Active route

```
Codes: P—Passive, A—Active, U—Update, Q—Query, R—Reply,
   r—Reply status

A 10.1.6.0/24, 0 successors, FD is 264000, Q
    1 replies, active 00:02:05, query-origin: Local origin
         via 10.1.1.2 (Infinity/Infinity), r, Serial1
```

The lowercase **r** in the last line tells us that router A is waiting on a response to its query about the 10.1.6.0/24 network from router B. The next step, then, is to TELNET to router B and see why it's not answering A's query. On router B, we see

```
A 10.1.6.0/24, 0 successors, FD is 263000, Q
    1 replies, active 00:02:10, query-origin: Local origin
         via 10.1.2.1 (Infinity/Infinity), Serial0
Remaining replies:
         via 10.1.3.1, r, Serial1
```

Router B is waiting on router D, 10.1.3.1, to answer. (Router A, 10.1.2.1, has already answered; note that it doesn't have the lowercase r in its output.) If we TELNET to router D and check its topology table, we see

```
A 10.1.6.0/24, 0 successors, FD is 262000, Q
    1 replies, active 00:02:10, query-origin: Local origin
         via 10.1.4.1 (Infinity/Infinity), r, Serial0
```

Router D is waiting on router E for an answer. Because router E is directly attached to the network that is declared SIA on router A, the problem is most likely between routers D and E. We would now investigate the condition of router E to determine whether it has enough memory and processing power to answer the queries. We would also check the state and condition of the link between routers D and E, as a high error rate or a large number of dropped packets can cause EIGRP to malfunction on this link.

In general, good design will prevent most SIAs from ever occurring. The best thing to do when you have an SIA problem is to chase the SIA to its source, check the area for routers in trouble and links that are failing, and fix what you find. Then start looking at how you can change the design of your network to improve its odds of surviving a route being marked active. See Chapter 3 for ideas.

Duplicate Router IDs

Not many people realize that EIGRP uses router IDs at all, so it comes as a surprise even to EIGRP veterans that duplicate router IDs can cause problems. EIGRP uses router IDs to identify the source of an external route and to prevent routing loops to external destinations; a router running EIGRP will not accept an external route sourced from the same router ID as its local ID.

For instance, in the network in Figure 4.5, if routers A and C have the same router ID, neither will accept external routes sourced from the other. The result would be that router A doesn't have the 10.1.6.0/24 network in its routing or topology tables, and router C wouldn't have the 10.1.3.0/24 network in its routing or topology tables. This problem is difficult not only to detect—you would have to note that all the routes missing out of the topology table on both of these routers are externals—but also to verify and to remedy.

Until recently, in order to find router A's router ID in this network, you would need to check the topology table on router B or another neighbor router for externals sourced by router A. If router A isn't originating any external routes, you would need to set up a static or other route to redistribute so you could see the entry in router B's topology table.

Chapter 4: EIGRP Troubleshooting

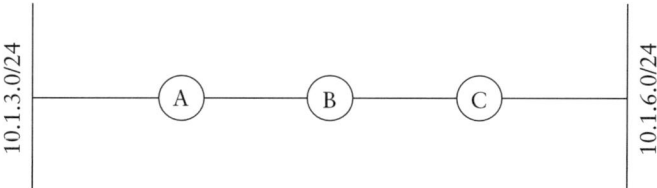

Figure 4.5 Duplicate router IDs

```
B#show ip eigrp topology 10.1.3.0 255.255.255.0


IP-EIGRP topology entry for 10.1.3.0/24

10.1.2.2 (Ethernet0), from 10.1.2.2, Send flag is 0x0
     Composite metric is (307200/281600), Route is
       External
     Vector metric:
       Minimum bandwidth is 10000 Kbit
       Total delay is 2000 microseconds
       Reliability is 0/255
       Load is 1/255
       Minimum MTU is 1500
       Hop count is 2
     External data:
       Originating router is 10.1.2.2
       AS number of route is 0
       External protocol is Static, external metric is 0
       Administrator tag is 0 (0x00000000)
```

The `Originating Router` field in the external data portion of the preceding topology table entry identifies the router ID of the router that originated this external route.

The router's ID is displayed in the output of `show ip eigrp topology`.

```
B#show ip eigrp topology
IP-EIGRP Topology Table for AS(100)/ID(10.1.2.2)
 . . . .
```

Beyond this point, an undocumented event log records the receipt of external routes with a duplicate router ID:

```
C#show ip eigrp event
Event information for AS 100:
. . . .
1   00:00:03.171 Ignored Route, dup router: 10.1.3.0
    10.1.2.2
2       00:00:03.171 Ignored route, neighbor info: 10.1.4.1
    Serial1
. . . .
```

The first of these two messages gives you the ignored route, followed by the ID of the router that originated it. The second message gives you information about which neighbor and interface the route was received from. Again, this event log is completely undocumented, and Cisco will not provide you with any help deciphering the output or purpose of any of the entries in the log.

How do multiple routers end up with the same router ID? EIGRP chooses its router ID on Cisco routers in the same way that other protocols, such as OSPF and BGP, do.

- The highest IP address configured on a loop-back interface is chosen as the router ID. A loop-back interface in a Cisco router is a logical interface that always has an "up/up" state.

- If there are no loop-back interfaces, the highest IP address on any interface that is operational is chosen.

After having chosen its router ID, EIGRP will not change it, even if the interface with that IP address is removed from the router and reconfigured elsewhere. Configuring loop-back interfaces on every router with the same IP address would definitely cause this problem, so you need to be careful when using loop-back interfaces all numbered the same, for anycast, in a multicast environment. The only way to resolve duplicate router IDs is to change the configuration of the routers as needed and to restart the EIGRP routing process.

Failure to Converge

It is extremely unusual for a network running EIGRP to simply fail to converge, but it is possible. A network meltdown is generally caused by a large number of parallel paths combined with a large trauma or a partial router failure; routers can fail in such a way that they cause more damage to the network than simply not passing traffic.

The best course of action to take when dealing with a network that is failing to converge is to first stabilize the network and then start trying to figure out what caused the convergence failure. To stabilize a network that won't converge, you should simplify the network and isolate misbehaving routers.

Simplifying the Network

The first action you should take when trying to stabilize a network that won't converge is to simplify the network as much as possible.

- Reduce the complexity of fully meshed areas in your network so that only one or two paths through hub routers remain. Doing so will add hops to the path IP traffic must take but can dramatically reduce the amount of work EIGRP must do to converge.

- Eliminate any backup links between remote locations and the center of the network. If these backup links haven't been designed properly, they will appear to be alternative paths through the network to EIGRP and can greatly increase the workload on routers attempting to converge.

In general, you should stop running EIGRP on as many redundant links as you can until the network converges. It isn't necessary to shut these redundant links off; it's often faster and easier to simply use the `passive-interface` command within EIGRP to stop EIGRP from building neighbor relationships on those links.

Isolate Misbehaving Routers

Once the redundancy in the network has been reduced or removed, actions can be taken to isolate routers that are misbehaving, such as not answering queries, from the network and to provide EIGRP with the stability it needs to converge. Routers that have been involved in a traumatic network event may be low on memory, running very high processor utilization, or otherwise be unstable. Use the techniques described in the section Stuck in Active Routes to chase down routers in trouble. Once you've found them, use distribution lists to reduce to the minimum possible the number of routes they must deal with and the number of queries they must generate.

Diagnose the Event

Once the network is stable, it's time to start from the beginning and try to discover what event caused the problem in the first place. Often, this task will be impossible without a lot of baseline data, such as how much processor and memory each router in your network normally has free (or used), what the normal traffic levels on each link in the network are, and other such information.

Most network meltdowns are caused by a combination of poor design—or a network out of control or not designed at all—marginal or failing links, and marginal or failing routers. The best thing to do is to clean up the network as much as possible and then work through the design of the network, using Chapter 3 as a baseline.

In a well-designed, well-maintained network, EIGRP can provide huge salability without any of these problems. The best approach to troubleshooting an EIGRP network is to design it correctly from the beginning.

Glossary

access layer In a network, a group of routers responsible for providing connectivity to external or remote sites. CPU-intensive functions, such as packet filtering, are implemented in the access layer of a network.

access rate The maximum speed, in bits per second, at which a network node may transmit or receive information over a physical link.

acknowledgment A packet or a frame used to indicate that information has been received.

active In EIGRP, a route is considered to be active state if a change in the topology has caused it not to have a successor available. During active processing, EIGRP attempts to find an alternative path to the target network.

AD (administrative distance) The relative weight assigned to each routing protocol by a Cisco router; used to select the preferred route if two or more protocols have the same prefix.

address summarization The method used to aggregate routing information into shorter prefixes.

AS (autonomous system) A group of routers with a common routing policy. In general, an autonomous system operates under a single administrative control and may use one or more interior gateway protocols.

ATM (asynchronous transfer mode) A data-switching technology that uses fixed-length (53-byte) cells.

autosummarization The automatic aggregation of routing information at major network boundaries, where the addressing in a network changes from one classful network to another.

bandwidth The speed (in bits per second) available for data transmission in a particular link or media. Also used by EIGRP as a component of the metric for path determination.

BGP (Border Gateway Protocol) A routing protocol used for interdomain routing.

broadcast The transmission mode used to send information to all the destinations in a particular network or subnet.

BUS (broadcast and unknown server) In ATM LANE, the network component that is used to forward traffic destined to a multicast or broadcast address. BUS also floods information addressed to an unknown destination.

CDP (Cisco Discovery Protocol) The media-independent protocol Cisco equipment uses to discover neighboring devices.

CEF (Cisco Express Forwarding) The switching method used for layer 3 forwarding in Cisco equipment.

CIR (committed information rate) The guaranteed bandwidth associated with a frame relay PVC.

classful/classless A classful protocol does not advertise a mask in its routing updates; a classless protocol does, making it capable of advertising supernets. In general, IP addresses are divided into classes (A, B, and C). A network that corresponds to one of these major classes is considered classful.

convergence time The time between a change in a network and the moment when all the nodes have been made aware of it and processed the information.

core layer In a network, a group of routers that represents the backbone. In general, routers in the core layer are expected to have complete routing information and to carry large amounts of traffic.

default network The network used to send all traffic for which an explicit route does not exist.

default route The route used to forward traffic for which an explicit route does not exist.

delay The time required for information to travel between two points in a network.

discontiguous network An addressing scheme in which the components of a major network (Class A, B, or C) are physically and logically separated by addresses corresponding to a different major network.

distance vector protocol A routing protocol that propagates information by announcing all its known destinations to local neighbors. EIGRP, IGRP, and RIP are examples of distance vector protocols.

distribution layer In a network, a group of routers that connects the access layer to the core layer. In general, common services, such as authentication and databases, are located at the distribution layer.

DLCI (data link connection identifier) A value that identifies a PVC or an SVC in a frame relay network.

DUAL (Diffusing Update Algorithm) The algorithm used to find loop-free paths through a network.

dual-homed remotes Remote routers that have connections to two different access-layer routers.

external routes Routes carried by a routing protocol that originated outside its domain. These routes may have been originated by other protocols or from static routes.

feasible distance (FD) The calculated metric, or cost, to a destination as reported by the successor.

feasible successor (FS) An EIGRP neighbor that advertised a guaranteed loop-free path to a destination but is not the best path.

floating static route A manually configured static route that is assigned a higher administrative distance than a dynamically learned route, so that if the dynamic route is removed from the routing table, the static route is installed.

frame relay WAN (wide area network) technology that allows a single physical link from a router to be shared by connections to multiple remote sites, using DLCIs.

HDLC (high-level data link control) A bit-oriented synchronous data link-layer protocol developed by ISO. HDLC specifies a data encapsulation method on synchronous serial links, using frame characters and checksums.

hello interval The frequency with which a router sends hello packets out of an interface. A hello interval has default values, based on interface type, or can be manually configured per interface.

hierarchy The method of network design that uses a layered approach based on function. Typically, the hierarchy comprises the core, distribution, and access layers.

holddown The amount of time a routing protocol will wait once it has lost a path to a specific destination before accepting another path of equal or higher cost to that destination.

hold time How long a router will wait without hearing an EIGRP packet from a neighbor before declaring that neighbor down. The hold time defaults to three times the hello interval but can be manually set per interface.

IGRP (Interior Gateway Routing Protocol) The Cisco-proprietary distance vector protocol that was the predecessor of EIGRP.

incremental updates The technique of sending only the changes instead of full information in routing updates to neighbors. EIGRP uses incremental updates.

information hiding A network design method that limits the information known by routers in the network to that necessary to properly route traffic; typically implemented through the use of summarization and/or route filtering.

IS-IS (Intermediate System to Intermediate System) A link state protocol defined by the International Standards Organization, originally to support OSI networks. Integrated IS-IS expanded IS-IS to include the ability to support IP networks.

ISDN (integrated services digital network) The connection method typically used for dialing over digital services.

K value Defines a multiplier for the components of the EIGRP metric in the metric calculation. Defaults to include only the minimum bandwidth and delay components but can be manually set to include load and reliability, using the `metric-weight` command. Not recommended.

LAN (local area network) A high-speed, low-error data network covering a relatively small geographic area. LAN standards specify cabling and signaling at the physical and data link layers of the OSI model. Ethernet, FDDI, and Token Ring are typical LAN technologies.

LANE (LAN emulation) Technology that permits asynchronous transfer mode (ATM) networks to function as a LAN backbone. LANE appears to the network layer to operate as an Ethernet and Token Ring LANs through the use of address mapping, emulated broadcast support, and so on.

link state protocol A routing protocol that floods information throughout an area and then performs a shortest-path first algorithm, such as Dijkstra's algorithm, on the received information to create a shortest-path tree with itself as root. IS-IS and OSPF are both widely used link state protocols.

load The EIGRP metric component that describes the level of traffic passing across a link. The value is encoded as $x/255$; the larger the value of x, the greater the amount of traffic. Load is not used in the metric calculation by default, but it may be enabled via the `metric-weight` command.

MAC (media access control) address A link-layer address that identifies which device on a LAN is the source or destination of a packet. Also known as the hardware address.

metric The measurement a routing protocol uses to determine which path is best to reach a particular target. In EIGRP, the metric potentially comprises delay, minimum bandwidth, load, and reliability. By default, only delay and minimum bandwidth are used.

MTU (maximum transmission unit) The maximum size of a packet supported across a particular link/interface.

multicast The addressing method—at both the link and the network layer—that allows a single packet to be received and processed by more than one device at a time.

multipoint The type of frame relay network that allows multiple devices to connect using the same network-layer address range, as if sharing a subnet, but that uses separate permanent virtual circuits (PVCs) to reach each remote device.

NBMA (nonbroadcast multiaccess) A network that supports the connection to multiple devices to the same layer 3 network but doesn't support the delivery of broadcast or multicast packets. Frame relay multipoint interfaces and X.25 networks are examples of NBMA networks.

neighbor A relationship whereby routers running the same routing protocol share one or more links.

ODR (on-demand routing) The mechanism that allows routes to be received from other routers via Cisco Discovery Protocol (CDP).

Offset list The method used to change the metric routes sent to or received from selected neighbors by increasing the delay component of the metric.

OSPF (Open Shortest Path First) A widely deployed hierarchical, standards-based link state interior gateway protocol.

pacing interval The method EIGRP uses to determine how quickly EIGRP packets can be sent out of an interface. By default, EIGRP will use no more than half the defined bandwidth of an interface.

PAP/CHAP passive The normal, stable state of a route in EIGRP.

point-to-point link The type of link that connects only two devices. HDLC links are typical point-to-point links.

point-to-point subinterfaces A type of frame relay configuration that emulates point-to-point links on a frame relay network. Each point-to-point subinterface connects only two devices across a PVC.

poison reverse The technique that occurs when a router, on receiving an advertisement for a destination through a given interface, readvertises that destination through the same interface as unreachable. Poison reverse prevents count-to-infinity routing loops in distance vector protocols.

PRI (primary rate interface) An ISDN interface with 23 data bearer (B) channels and an aggregate bandwidth equal to a T1.

PVC (permanent virtual circuit) A virtual circuit—a logical circuit multiplexed onto a series of physical links—permanently connected between two points on a network.

quality of service Providing service based on latency, jitter, bandwidth, or traffic-loss requirements to applications running over the network.

query In EIGRP, a request by one router to its peers for alternative paths to a given destination.

query scope The number of routers involved in a query event; the number of routers that will receive a query and be forced to reply before the router that originated the queries is answered.

redistribution Distributing information about reachable destinations learned through one routing protocol into another routing protocol.

redundancy Providing multiple paths through a network so a given number of failures will not prevent traffic from being delivered.

reliability A metric, measured as a factor of packets lost between the peers; the reliability of a link between two EIGRP peers.

reliable multicast A system of reliably sending multicast packets between two routers.

reported distance (RD) The distance, or cost, of reaching a given destination through a router as reported by that router. The link between the reporting router and the receiving router is not included in the reported distance.

RIP (Routing Information Protocol) Based on the Bellman-Ford algorithm, a distance vector protocol that uses periodic full updates between peers to provide routing information.

route filtering Preventing a router from advertising given destinations to its neighbors.

router ID A unique identifier for a router.

RTO (retransmission timeout) The amount of time a router running EIGRP will wait before retrying an unacknowledged transmission.

SIA (Stuck in Active) An EIGRP route that has been in active state longer than allowed by the Stuck in Active timer; typically, 3 minutes.

SMDS (switched multimegabit data service) A wide area network service similar to frame relay but higher in speed and capable of broadcast.

split horizon The technique of a router's not advertising a destination through an interface being used to reach it.

SRTT (smooth round-trip time) The amount of time previously taken for a peer to acknowledge transmissions.

stub In a network, a point beyond which there is no connectivity back toward the network's core; for instance, a remote site with only a few directly connected networks.

successor The EIGRP peer being used as the next hop toward a given destination.

summarization The process of consolidating several longer-prefix destination advertisements into one shorter-prefix advertisement.

topology The logical (IP or network layer) layout of the network.

topology database A repository of information a router knows about the network's topology. Used by EIGRP.

traffic aggregation Combining several lower-speed links onto one higher-speed link.

transit paths Links through which traffic passes en route to its destination; traffic doesn't terminate (or stop) on a transit link but just passes through.

unicast A packet transmitted from one host to another single host.

Update Information about destination and path and transmitted to a neighbor.

variance The amount of difference allowed between unequal-cost paths while still load sharing.

VLANs Virtual logical networks created on top of a set of physical links using local area network media; on WAN links, these are called PVCs.

VLSM (variable-length subnet masks) Having multiple prefix lengths within a single major network.

WAN (wide area network) Typically, a network that traverses long distances (outside of a campus environment).

Recommended Reading

Throughout this book, we have covered details on EIGRP, from the fundamentals to network design. Other aspects of networking are also important for you to understand in order to deploy scalable and robust networks.

The following two books present a broad view of protocol functionality and network design. We recommend that you use them both in conjunction with this one.

Perlman, Radia, *Interconnections: Bridges, Routers, Switches and Internetworking*, 2d ed., Reading, MA: Addison Wesley Longman, 2000.

Retana, Alvaro, Don Slice, and Russ White, *Advanced IP Network Design*, Indianapolis, IN: Cisco Press, 1999.

Index

A

ABRs (Area Border Routers), 8
Access layer, 39
Access lists as distribution lists
  extended, 32–33
  standard, 31–32
Acknowledgment, 10
Active
  routes marked as, 19
  routes staying, 102–104
Active routes, stuck in, 101–104
AD (administrative distance), 26
Addresses
  broadcast, 7
  multicast, 5
  summarization, 37
Administrative distances, 82–84
Administrative tag, 26
ADs (administrative distances), 82–84
Aggregation, traffic, 38
Algorithm, Diffusing Update, 1
AS (autonomous system), 23
  multiple, 48–49, 87–89
  number, 25
ASBRs (Autonomous System Border Routers), 8
Asymmetrical routing, 57–58
Autonomous systems, multiple, 48–49, 87–89
Autosummarization, 28–29, 42

B

Backup strategies, dial, 74–76
Bandwidth, 4
Bandwidth consumption, limiting, 12–13
Bandwidth statements, frame relay and, 62–64
BGP (Border Gateway Protocol), 9
BRI (basic rate interface), 66
Broadcast address, 7
Broadcast queue, frame-relay, 72–74
BUS (broadcast and unknown server), 98

C

CDIR (classless interdomain routing), 25
CDP (Cisco Discovery Protocol), 49
CEF (Cisco Express Forwarding), 57
CIR (committed information rate), 63, 65
Cisco routers, redistribution on, 27
Cisco's EIGRP (Enhanced Interior Gateway Routing Protocol), 1
Classful, 7
Commands, network, 23–25
Communication, one-way, 96–97
Configuration, EIGRP, 23–35
  distribution lists, 31–33
  hello and hold timers, 33–34
  logging neighbor status, 34
  passive interface, 34–35
  redistribution, 25–27
  running EIGRP, 23–25
  starting EIGRP, 23–25
  stub neighbors, 35
  summarization, 28–31
Converge, failure to, 107–108
Convergence time, 18
Count-to-infinity problem, 3, 18

D

Database, topology, 4
Default network, 59–62
Default route, 45, 60–62
Delay, 4
Design considerations, miscellaneous, 91–93
Design, network, 37–93
Dial backup strategies, 74–76
Dial issues, WAN and, 62–76
Dirty link, overburdened or, 100–101
Discontiguous subnets, 43
Distance vector protocols, 1–4
  metrics, 4
  updates, 2–4
Distribution layer, 38
Distribution lists, 31–33, 89
  extended access lists as, 32–33

standard access lists as, 31–32
Distribution. *See also* Redistribution
DLCI (data link connection identities), 64
DUAL (Diffusing Update Algorithm), 1, 13–17
Dual-homed remotes, 47, 67–69

E

EIGRP (Enhanced Interior Gateway Routing Protocol)
  basics of, 8–13
    limiting bandwidth consumption, 12–13
    neighbor relationships, 8–9
    reliable multicast, 9–12
  compared to other protocols, 6–8
  configuration, 23–35
  deciding where to use, 22
  foundation: Diffusing Update Algorithm (DUAL), 13–17
  fundamentals, 1–22
  multiple, 87–89
  network design, 37–93
  redistributing metrics into, 27
  running, 23–25
  starting, 23–25
  uses incremental updates, 3
Events, diagnosing, 108

F

FD (feasible distance), 14
Feasible successor, queries with no, 20–21
Filtering, route, 45–47, 89–90
Floating static route, 46
Frame relay
  and bandwidth statements, 62–64
  broadcast queue, 72–74
  point-to-point subinterfaces, 9
FS (feasible successor), 14, 17

H

HDLC (high-level data link control), 9
Hello
  interval, 70
  packet, 9
  timers, 33–34
Hold timers, 9, 33–34
Horizon, split, 17–22

I

IDs
  duplicate router, 104–106
  process, 25
IGRP (Interior Gateway Routing Protocol), 1–3
  in same autonomous system, 85–87
Incremental updates, 3
Information hiding, 39
Interfaces
  changing metric components on, 50–52
  multipoint, 64–67
  passive, 34–35
  See also Subinterfaces
Interval, hello, 70
IS-IS (Intermediate System to Intermediate System), 5–6, 8

K

K values, changing, 53–54

L

LAN (local area network), 9
LANE (LAN emulation), 98
Link state protocols, 1–2, 5–6
Links
  multipoint, 9
  overburdened or dirty, 100–101
  point-to-point, 9
Links and SIAs, low-speed NBMA, 69–71
Lists
  distribution, 31–33, 89
  extended access lists as distribution, 32–33
  offset, 52–53
  standard access lists as distribution, 31–32
Lists as distribution lists, standard access, 31–32
Load, 4

M

MAC (media access control), 9
Metric components, changing on interface, 50–52
Metrics, 4, 15–16, 27
MTU (maximum transmission unit), 15, 26

Index

Multicast address, 5
Multicast-only between two routers, 99–100
Multicast, reliable, 9–12
Multipoint interfaces and subinterfaces, 64–67
Multipoint links, 9
Mutual redistribution
  at multiple points between two networks, 81–82
  at single point, 80–81

N

NBMA links and SIAs, low-speed, 69–71
NBMA (nonbroadcast multiaccess), 69
Neighbor relationships, 8–9
  problems with, 95–101
Neighbor status, logging, 34
Neighbors, stub, 35
Network command, 23–25
Network design, 37–93
  minimizing query range, 41–50
  miscellaneous design considerations, 91–93
  network topology, 37–40
  path selection issues, 50–62
  redistribution issues, 76–90
  WAN and dial issues, 62–76
Network statement and routes, 27
Network topology, 37–40
  hierarchy, 38–39
  redundancy, 39–40
Networks
default, 59–62
  multiple, 82
  mutual redistribution at multiple points between two, 81–82
  simplifying, 107
  See also Subnets
Numbers, AS (autonomous system), 25

O

ODR (on-demand routing), 49, 69
Offset lists, 52–53
One-way communication between two routers, 96–97
One-way redistribution, 80
OSPF (Open Shortest Path First), 5–6

P

Packet, hello, 9
Passive
  entries marked as, 19
  interfaces, 34–35
Path selection issues, 50–62
  asymmetrical routing, 57–58
  changing K values, 53–54
  changing metric components on interface, 50–52
  default routing strategy, 58–62
  offset lists, 52–53
  variance, 55–57
Paths, transit, 39
Point-to-point links, 9
Point-to-point subinterfaces, 64
  frame relay, 9
Process ID, 25
Protocols
  distance vector, 1–4
  EIGRP compared to other protocols, 6–8
  link state, 1–2, 5–6
  multiple routing, 49–50
PVC (permanent virtual circuit), 64–65

Q

Quality of service, 39
Queries, 8
  ending of, 21–22
  with no feasible successor, 20–21
  split horizon and, 17–22
Query ranges, minimizing, 41–50
  multiple autonomous systems, 48–49
  multiple routing protocols, 49–50
  route filtering, 45–47
  stub routers, 47–48
  summarization, 42–45
Query scopes, 41
Queues, frame-relay broadcast, 72–74

R

RD (reported distance), 14
Redistributed routes, source of, 84–90
  IGRP in same autonomous system, 85–87
  multiple EIGRP autonomous systems, 87–89
  route filtering, 89–90

Redistribution, 25–27
    caveats, 27
    on Cisco routers, 27
    externals and internals, 26–27
    forms of, 80–82
        administrative distances, 82–84
        mutual redistribution at multiple points between two networks, 81–82
        mutual redistribution at single point, 80–81
        mutual redistribution between multiple networks at multiple points, 82
        one-way redistribution, 80
        source of redistributed routes, 84–90
    issues, 76–90
        forms of redistribution, 80–82
        general issues, 77–80
    mutual, 82
    one-way, 80
Redistribution at single point, mutual, 80–81
Relationships
    neighbor, 8–9
    problems with neighbor, 95–101
Reliability, 4, 15
Remotes, dual-homed, 47, 67–69
RIP (Routing Information Protocol), 1, 3
Route filtering, 42, 45–47, 89–90
Route summarization, 42
Router IDs, duplicate, 104–106
Routers
    isolating misbehaving, 107–108
    multicast-only between two, 99–100
    one-way communication between two, 96–97
    redistribution on Cisco, 27
    stub, 47–48
    unicast-only between two, 97–98
Routes
    active, 19
    default, 45, 60–62
    floating static, 46
    going active, 101–102
    network statement and, 27
    source of redistributed, 84–90
    staying active, 102–104
    stuck in active, 101–104
Routing, asymmetrical, 57–58

Routing protocols, multiple, 49–50
Routing strategy, default, 58–62
    default network, 59–60
    default network or default route, 61–62
    default route, 60–61
RTO (retransmission timeout), 10–11
Running EIGRP, 23–25

S

Scope, query, 41
Service, quality of, 39
SIA (Stuck in Active), 21, 101–102, 104
SIAs, low-speed NBMA links and, 69–71
SMDS (switched multimegabit data service), 63–64, 66, 70
Split horizon
    NBMA (non broadcast multiaccess) and, 72
    and queries, 17–22
SRTT (smooth round-trip time), 10–11
Starting EIGRP, 23–25
Stub neighbors, 35
Stub routers, 47–48
Subinterfaces
    frame relay point-to-point, 9
    multipoint interfaces and, 64–67
    point-to-point, 64
Subnets, discontiguous, 43
Successor, 14
Summarization, 6, 42–45
    address, 37
    configuring, 28–31
        autosummarization, 28–29
        manual summarization, 29–31
    route, 42

T

Tag, administrative, 26
Time, convergence, 18
Timers
    hello, 33–34
    hold, 9, 33–34
Topology, 7
    database, 4
    network, 37–40
Traffic aggregation, 38
Transit paths, 39

Index

Troubleshooting, 95–108
  duplicate router IDs, 104–106
  failure to converge, 107–108
    diagnosing events, 108
    isolating misbehaving routers, 107–108
    simplifying networks, 107
  one-way communication between two routers, 96–97
    multicast-only between two routers, 99–100
    overburdened or dirty-link, 100–101
    unicast-only between two routers, 97–98
  problems with neighbor relationships, 95–101
  stuck in active routes, 101–104

U

Unicast-only between two routers, 97–98
Updates, incremental, 3

V

Variance, 55–57
VLANs, 39
VLSM (variable-length subnet masks), 77

W

WAN (wide area network), 38
  and dial issues, 62–76
    dial backup strategies, 74–76
    dual-homed remotes, 67–69
    frame relay and bandwidth statements, 62–64
    frame-relay broadcast queue, 72–74
    low-speed NBMA links and SIAs, 69–71
    multipoint interfaces and subinterfaces, 64–67
    NBMA (non broadcast multiaccess) and split horizon, 72
    point-to-point subinterfaces, 64
  links, 62

✧ THE ADDISON–WESLEY NETWORKING BASICS SERIES

Focused and Concise Hands-On Guides for Networking Professionals

The Addison-Wesley Networking Basics Series is a set of concise, hands-on guides to today's key computer networking technologies and protocols. Each volume in the series covers a focused topic, presenting the steps required to implement and work with specific technologies and tools in network programming, administration, and security. Providing practical, problem-solving information, these books are written by practicing professionals who have mastered complex network challenges.

0-201-37951-1

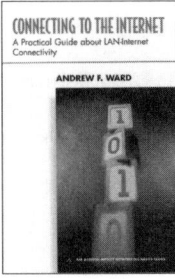
0-201-37956-2

0-201-61584-3

0-201-37924-4

0-201-60448-5

0-201-37957-0

0-201-43320-6

0-201-65773-2

Please visit our Web site at
http://www.aw.com/cseng/networkingbasics/
for more information on these titles.

Addison-Wesley Professional

How to Register Your Book

Register this Book
Visit: **http://www.aw.com/cseng/register**
Enter the ISBN*
Then you will receive:
- Notices and reminders about upcoming author appearances, tradeshows, and online chats with special guests
- Advanced notice of forthcoming editions of your book
- Book recommendations
- Notification about special contests and promotions throughout the year

*The ISBN can be found on the copyright page of the book

Visit our Web site
http://www.aw.com/cseng

When you think you've read enough, there's always more content for you at Addison-Wesley's web site. Our web site contains a directory of complete product information including:
- Chapters
- Exclusive author interviews
- Links to authors' pages
- Tables of contents
- Source code

You can also discover what tradeshows and conferences Addison-Wesley will be attending, read what others are saying about our titles, and find out where and when you can meet our authors and have them sign your book.

We encourage you to patronize the many fine retailers who stock Addison-Wesley titles. Visit our online directory to find stores near you.

Contact Us via Email
cepubprof@awl.com
Ask general questions about our books.
Sign up for our electronic mailing lists.
Submit corrections for our web site.

cepubeditors@awl.com
Submit a book proposal.
Send errata for a book.

cepubpublicity@awl.com
Request a review copy for a member of the media interested in reviewing new titles.

registration@awl.com
Request information about book registration.

Addison-Wesley Professional
One Jacob Way, Reading, Massachusetts 01867 USA
TEL 781-944-3700 • FAX 781-942-3076